T0196313

pagan time

pagan
time

AN AMERICAN CHILDHOOD

micah perks

COUNTERPOINT

BERKELEY

Library of Congress Cataloging-in-Publication Data
Perks, Micah.
Pagan time : an American childhood / Micah Perks.
p. cm.

ISBN: 978-1-58243-539-8

1. Perks, Micah—Childhood and youth. 2. Communal living—
New York (State)—Adirondack Mountains Region. 3. Adirondack
Mountains Region (N.Y.)—Social life and customs. 4. Family—New York
(State)—Adirondack Mountains Region. 5. Novelists, American—
20th century—Biography. 6. Adirondack Mountains Region (N.Y.)—
Biography. 7. English teachers—United States—Biography.   I. Title.
ps3566.e691487 z477 2001
813'.54—dc21   2001028893

Book design by Mark McGarry, Texas Type & Book Works
Set in Stempel Garamond

Printed in the United States of America

COUNTERPOINT
2560 Ninth Street
Suite 318
Berkeley, CA 94710

www.counterpointpress.com

For Naomi, Joe, John and Bekah.
Though their costumes change, their generosity
and good humor remain.

But I reckon I got to light out for the Territory ahead of the rest, because Aunt Sally she's going to adopt me and sivilize me and I can't stand it. I been there before.

MARK TWAIN

Do you know what you really want? I'll tell you. You want to be took home and took care of. And I guess that's all there is to say.

EDITH WHARTON

CHAPTER ONE

how to get there

THE TIME of my childhood was the nineteen sixties.

I know what you're thinking—marijuana, free love, Woodstock and Watts and Vietnam. Because you know the sixties. You were young then, or raising children, or not even born yet, but in any case, you've seen it on television.

The sixties are black-and-white reruns—Kennedy rearing back in the convertible, King falling into the balcony, Malcolm X colliding with the podium; a grainy leap from spaceship to moon; white cops not holding back German shepherds as they attack black protesters.

Or the sixties are finger-painted in psychedelics—the color of an acid trip, of blue-tinted granny glasses, of long blond hair and afros entwined with rainbow love beads.

Or the sixties are peace signs in a commercial for a fast food chain, bell-bottoms on a Barbie doll. The sixties are a retro fashion statement, a cliché, a quaint cul-de-sac, over and done with, let's move on.

Wait.

You're right, but there's more to it than that. I'm ready to tell you secrets. I want you to see. This desire has been pressing for a long time. Sometimes it seems like I've spent my life searching for the words that will open my childhood for you.

I'm in ninth grade—you are a handsome senior driving me home. You're wearing chinos, a polo shirt and loafers. Rain is tapping on the roof, sliding over the windshield. You ask me where I lived before, and I begin to explain. It was a school for disturbed adolescents. But I wasn't disturbed. Well, we were all a little disturbed, but not in a bad way. Actually, it was more like a commune. More of a farm, really....

You laugh nervously, say, Gosh.

I close my mouth and watch the wipers control the rain.

Or, I'm just out of college, in a field, sharing a sleeping bag with you. This time you have beige hair, blue eyes, a snub nose, callused hands. We've just made love for the first time. Everything glows—red fire, green fireflies, white moon. You tell me about racing bicycles, about growing up rich and Quaker in Philadelphia. I try to tell you about the valley school.

You say, I'm sorry, that sounds rough.

I say, That was the best part of my life (best is not quite accurate, but I don't know what other word to use).

We lie on our backs, mummied in the sleeping bag, close but not touching.

It's always the same—even as I'm trying to use my story to knock down the wall between us, I can see that I'm turning myself into a freak, my childhood a sideshow.

Let me try again.

In my time, in my place, a valley surrounded by thousands of acres of dark trees, we would join hands to create an Eden.

This is an old story. My mother could have been Adam, God's chosen one, riotous, keeper of harmony. If my mother is Adam, then my father is Lilith, Adam's first wife. Lilith was God's first mistake, a rule breaker, a seducer. Before God even finished patting Lilith together out of mud, she had wriggled out of His grasp. In the old stories, Lilith lights out for the territories, alone.

But what if Adam and Lilith attempt a daring escape together? In darkest night while He sleeps, they hoist each other over Eden's wall, swim the wide, slow-moving river. They stand on the far shore, trailing water weeds. It's their turn to create. Now what?

It goes on like this. If my mother is Natty Bumppo, my father is Chingachgook, last of the Mohicans. Or, they could be Ishmael and Queequeg, making passionate love on the night before setting sail on the *Pequod.* If my father is Huckleberry Finn, escape artist, liar, my mother is Jim, so angelically maternal you have to wonder what's underneath. Or, my parents are double Thoreaus without the desire for silence. Or, those two old Shaker women, who swore they flew to the moon in their rocking chairs, singing all the while, despite the lack of oxygen, *When we find ourselves in a place just right, we will be in the valley of love and delight.*

Or they are immigrants, pioneers. Or pilgrims. There would be sun, smacking sails, creaking wood, the plash of grey waves. Dressed in somber wool, my pilgrim parents face forward, imagining the new world. My mother's smile is serene, she is making plans for the amelioration of the unknown. But what is my father imagining? His own coronation? A mutiny? Or is he just happy to be getting the hell out of Dodge? And what kind of an Eden results from the imagination of a people whose first instinct is escape?

Maybe it's as simple as this. Two children begin a block tower. Take turns, steady, steady. How high will it go? How long until one child turns clumsy, or bored, or simply can no longer resist the urge to watch it teeter and fall?

Still, in the moment of placing that first block, in the moment of childhood, or of setting out on a great adventure, there is a feeling that transcends all contradiction. Remember that feeling, that shiver in your chest, as if anything were possible? In my childhood everyone I knew seemed to be walking around with that shiver I won't call hope.

I'll just tell you how to get there.

Leave the cities, the towns, drive for half a day, the never-ending curves churning your stomach, the trees pressing tighter and tighter against the narrow roads, to the very eastern edge of the

Adirondack Mountains. This land was covered over and over by warm, shallow Cambrian seas and more recently by glacial ice; then the softer sediment was slowly scoured off, baring the grey, hard, billion-year-old rock, the ancient continent.

Here, the mountains are pressed against Lake Champlain by the western weight of trailers, snowmobiles, diners with Budweiser neon, rusty pickup trucks with gun racks, a wax museum, a house of horror, Santa's Workshop, Make Believe Land and Frontier Town, ramshackle forests and crumbling revolutionary war forts, the whole brooding mess that makes up the Adirondack park; to the east, a sharp fall down to the plush farmland of the Champlain Valley and the greener mountains of Vermont.

Turn onto the county road, one side a ridge of spruce and rock, the other a slide down to metal-colored water. Watch out for logging trucks, they careen past, shedding bark and branches. (Leonard Canal, a young trucker, lost his breaks right here, on the steepest slope of the road. He pumped them, slammed the horn, felt his truck rattling faster and faster. He decided to bail. He leapt, but this was a miscalculation. His rig ran him over. The logs burst off the flatbed, but the truck came to rest, unmolested, on the narrow shoulder.)

Turn right onto what the locals have begun to call Funny Farm Road. Drive over teeth-jarring washout and frost heave for miles. Say it's the late sixties, late June, so blue flag and daisies line the ditches. Your car plows through clusters of white butterflies, wings pumping like breath.

Pass an abandoned brown house. People say they found the old lady starved dead in there a few years back, been eating cat food all winter. Wearing layers of clothes against the cold, no running water so she stank bad. Now, she haunts the house. The hippie juvenile delinquents have broken all the windows.

Over a fragile iron bridge beside roaring twin waterfalls. A bluebird flies in front of your car. Take this as a good omen. Another one-lane, rusted bridge over a shallow creek. On the other side, a saw blade nailed to a wide pine tree is painted with an ancient Mexican hieroglyph of a water lily. It looks like a red heart pulled in two directions, surrounded by a black fence. The words *Valley Commune School* are painted underneath.

Up a small hill and down into the valley. The Algonquin used to hunt here in the summers but thought the land too harsh and never stayed long. In the nineteenth century there were iron miners on the ridge above, and in the valley, a few stubborn farmers worked the thin dirt between tree stumps; but miners and farmers have long since given up. Now, we're trying our hand.

Scotch Highland cows, all orange and hairy, toss wicked-looking horns beside a mess of peeling red barns. Opposite, a long cement building that looks like a basement, painted with brown dancing figures. Then the three red and yellow geodesic domes attached to A-frames up against the hill. Turn right at the barns, pull up the driveway past the flag poles—an English flag, a revolutionary war flag with a green snake that reads Don't Tread On Me, some strange yellow flag from a place no one ever heard of—all three smacking in the wind. The old farmhouse is a riot of yellow and red. There is a long chicken yard against the house. Past the chickens, the valley stretches up a hill to three painted teepees.

Does your heart do something funny when you see the school for the first time? There are mountains all around it, so it's like a cup—it might hold anything. Open the car door, smell balsam, mold, chicken shit.

Tour the dilapidated barns, walk through mud and cow manure in your good shoes, slap at blackflies; eat spaghetti in the roar of the communal dining hall, and now, nine at night, come up the hill to the log cabin with the founder and co-director of the school, my mother.

There's no moon. Insects brush your face, and our huge, panting Newfoundland dog drools on your pants. Although you can't tell in the dark, my mother is wearing jeans and a Mexican embroidered blouse, her brown hair in a braid down the back.

Pull the iron latch on the massive front door of the log cabin, door won't budge. My mother instructs you to use two hands. Yank, palms burn and the door wrenches open. In front of you is a wooden plaque with flowering vines and the words Love Never Faileth.

My mother says she'll be with you in a minute, she has a phone call to make, a student to talk to, she has to round us up, her two little girls. She puts water on for coffee, starts rummaging through the piles of papers stacked along the windowsills.

Inside the cabin, it is dim: the black floors and dark log walls soak up the light from the stained-glass lamps. For decor, my parents favor blue and red, antique, monumental. Red and blue for the dirty Oriental rug, antique for the clawfoot chairs, monumental for the fireplace, nine feet wide in the center of the house. Everything open, sleeping loft for us, no walls downstairs (although, as you will soon see, there's no easy exit. We children have to wrap a dishtowel over the sharp latch and pull together to open the front door). There's a long wooden table, wooden chairs, smoky mirrors, dust, mice. The whole place smells vaguely of rodent piss.

My mother calls for my father to entertain you.

My father, the co-director, sees surprise as the key ingredient to hospitality. Now, he comes striding around the fireplace in his eighteenth-century, Royal Navy uniform, swallow-tailed blue woolen coat with gold buttons, ruffled white shirt, white breeches, black knee boots, sword at hip, hair in a braid with a velvet ribbon. Welcome, my father says to you in his British accent. (Beware the fine linen intonation that makes you think of teacups, makes you think of Commander Scott, foot frozen off, dying at the South Pole, writing, *We mean to see the game through with a proper spirit*. It's not that it's fake, it's just that he can speak as authentically in a working-class accent.)

He bows, gives you a kiss on the mouth, offers chocolate-covered ants and pickled pigs feet that he keeps in jars on the counter. Care for a trotter?

Refuse politely, sit down at the table. My father downs handfuls of the chocolate ants, raises a dripping white foot over his mouth, pops it in, smacks his lips for effect.

He sighs, These people came down the road, right? They had on their regulation-issue hippie clothes, I mean they were psychedelic. These two buddies wanted to start a real hippie commune in the middle of Manhattan. So, we gave them some live chickens in a sack to take home with them. We let these fellas spend the night, right? They're in sleeping bags in the meeting room, with their chickens, and that dog there, Panda, lays herself across the doorway and falls asleep. One of the fellas says, Jesus Christ, it's a wild boar! The other one starts tapping out SOS in

Morse code on the ceiling. Panda snuffles in her sleep, and they think the boar is growing hungry. So, they can't stand it anymore. They make a dash for the window, throw themselves over the sill, rush for their car, lock all the doors. They take off for the city and never return. And they forgot their chickens.

My father raises his eyebrows at you: Are you like them, a coward, a fool? Or are you for real? Then he shrugs, laughs and offers rum. He puts music on the record player, old British sailing songs. "Row You Bully Boys Row." He lights the kerosene lamps. He shows you a framed poster of Geronimo, tells you he was my mother's great-grandfather, she's part Indian, don't you know.

Say, I thought she was Jewish.

Jews are all right, but a Jewish Indian, now that's something. My father laughs.

Teachers begin to drift up to the cabin, the door is left ajar, everyone moves to the living room, sits on the couch and chairs and floor, drinking rum. The teachers are in their twenties or early thirties, people who laugh often, talk loudly. Their emotions ripple in their voices and hands, you never know when someone will turn furious or weep. They are sitting in each other's laps, talking about their students, about their own childhoods, saying shockingly honest things about themselves and each other.

Upstairs in our sleeping loft, we children climb onto our dresser, hoist ourselves onto the beam above. Below us: the orange sunset poster above my bed that reads, Each Dawn is a New Beginning; on the bookshelf, my beloved paperback biographies—Amelia Earhart, the disappearing mystery, Helen Keller, who spent her childhood in a dark rage, Susan B. Anthony, who said, Failure is impossible; on the floor, a tangle of naked Barbies. We leap down to the mattress we have dragged underneath the beam.

My mother tells you about the school. Familiar phrases drift upstairs and hover slightly over our heads as we play: troubled teens, juvenile delinquents, learning disabilities, court orders, handicaps, heroin, marijuana, shooting up, the clap, the pill, overdose, training schools, overmedicated, delusional.

When the valley school began, my mother explains, the students were mostly severely disturbed, diagnosed with schizophrenia. We are moving towards working primarily with disturbed adolescents now, referred by the courts. She tells about some of their successes. Frankie, the little Italian one with the dark hair? She's hard to reach, but she's fallen in love with the farm, she even slept in a stall one night, snuggled up against a cow. Ann, she still spits and scratches once in a while, but she's great with little kids, she baby-sits.

My father turns on the 1812 Overture, pours more rum around, begins to recite Shakespeare in a wet and rolling voice. The water has boiled out of the kettle, unnoticed. We stick a GI Joe into the flame under the kettle, watch his fuzzy crew cut sizzle, his sensitive face melt.

Coyotes howl outside, moths throw themselves against the windows. We children are fencing with shish kebab sticks.

My father turns on the Beatles, sits near you, says, What about a place where everyone can do whatever they want? The only rule is, no one gets hurt. What would that place be like?

The conversations pool. The education here is revolutionary, there's little differentiation between teachers and students.

It's a community, a place for the students to unplug from the insane world, get their heads together, where they're safe to feel all their emotions.

The valley is like a bag cinched at both ends.

The goal is to have an ongoing self-sustaining community. We want to start a sawmill, there could be a pottery, we could produce all our own food.

Our children are growing up together, free from the suffocating values of mainstream society. They're being educated at the Little School, that's what we call it, a one-room schoolhouse we built at the edge of the valley. They follow their hearts, too.

Even more, we're changing the established order, questioning everything, loosening the bonds of nuclear families.

The artificial walls come tumbling down, between student and teacher, work and play, one marriage and another marriage.

Monogamy is something they teach us not to question, it scares them.

Rum spills on the rug, Paul McCartney sings "Let It Be," my father is looking at you intently, a half smile on his face. What does he mean by it? The mice scrabble over the beams above your heads, the talk is quick and slurred and sharp. A teacher and my father agree to stage a new war, the Irish against the British.

The teacher says, Maybe this time we can have a fair fight.

Whatever do you mean, Sir? my father says.

I mean you always get the charming alcoholic kids, and we always get the schizophrenics and women and children.

My father says, May I remind you, the only rule is, no one is allowed to get mad.

My father is looking at you again, calls to you from across the room, What do you think? No bullshit.

Everyone watches.

It's wild, you say. They're still watching you. (Are you a coward, a fool?) You say, I want to stay.

Laughter, clapping.

We children fall asleep on the Oriental rug. I can still feel the bristles on my cheek. I drift away, rocked by the circle of people around me, their buoyant conversation, their valentine to the near future, their certainty that failure is impossible.

CHAPTER TWO

and the walls became the world all around 1967–1968

DETROIT is glowing from over a thousand arson fires, San Francisco is glowing with love and it's the far end of August in the Adirondacks. There's this brief month, between blackfly season and the first frost, a month of summer that riots with life. Morning glories strangle Queen Anne's lace and goldenrod; monarch caterpillars consume milkweed in preparation for transformation and flight; dragonflies skim mosquitoes off the breeze; swallows eat the dragonflies. It's every creeping thing.

Me, I'm stalking bees. I'm a kid in cutoffs, my matted hair stuffed up in a rainbow-colored wool tam, mason jar under my arm. I mean to surprise the bees at flower work in the front garden of the main house. My feet are pressing mostly into cool, loose dirt, but also partly on orange and yellow marigolds, their broken stems sighing bitter marigold breath.

Something slips across my ankle. Beside my foot, a snake is swallowing a frog. I crouch down. The snake's jaws are unhinged, absurdly wide—the frog's head is all that's not inside the snake. The frog is quiet, eyes bulging, same with the snake. I pick up a stick and poke it. The garter snake serpentines away, frog still in mouth. I think that I may begin collecting dandelions and make dandelion wine and sell it to the students so that I can purchase Fire Balls, my favorite penny candy. Then I remember the bees.

I sneak towards a honeybee laboring on an orange marigold. I can see her sacks of pollen. She starts to rise, with her official hum. I scoop her up in my jar and cover the opening with my palm. The bee pings from side to side, its buzz making an echoey sound against the glass.

There's commotion across the road, by the duck and goose pen. I hear my father's laugh. I head over. There's been trouble with foxes. Nights on end, a fox kills our ducks. He doesn't eat them, just breaks their necks, for fun. Now, I see my father between the barn and the open door of the pen, posing for a photograph next to a thigh-high pile of white feathers, his chest puffed out comically, his rifle held stiffly at his side. My father is wearing what he wears when he is not in fencing mask or cricket uniform or mountain man costume: work boots, jeans, belt with turquoise Navajo buckle, Ben Franklin glasses, beribboned ponytail, rolled-up blue work shirt. (He never wears T-shirts. He doesn't care for his Popeye arms, the forearms wider than the biceps.)

When I walk closer, but not too close, I see the feathers are a mound of limp-necked ducks. A dead fox is draped like an orange handkerchief over the heap.

While I'm watching, a goose leaves the pen and teeters towards me, neck stretched out, snakelike. She's hissing, ready to nip. I face her down. If you bite me, my father will put you in a pot and cook you for dinner. The goose is not impressed; she's battle ready. My father yells at the goose, picks up a stick and chucks it at her. The stick boffs against her dusty side; she squawks and veers off. Warned you, I say.

I head into the main house to find my mother and show her my bee, show how my bare hand caps the jar, how oblivious I am to the threat of sting. I walk into the living room.

Someone's been messing with my dollhouse. I put down my jar and the bee rises, smokes towards the window, mistaking it for freedom. My miniature furniture is all messed up—the toilet is on top of the bed, the doll parents are unclothed and doing a sixty-nine on the kitchen table, the baby is in the fireplace. Then I notice the little girl doll is mummied in white string. Rage fills my heart. I know whose work this is. I punch open the screen door, march towards the bell.

The bell occupies a place of grandeur, right in the center of the valley, on top of a thirty-foot, three-tiered tower my father has built. I have never pulled this rope, and I look around, a little afraid. I yank cautiously, nothing happens. Then I remember the ruination. I give the rope all my weight and the old bell begins to clang. Everyone I know appears, heading towards the main house meeting room. I follow, nursing my outrage.

They take their shoes off at the door to the meeting room. No one has matching socks. The meeting room is an amphitheater covered in wall-to-ceiling green carpet. You would certainly notice oddity here—black plastic glasses askew, T-shirt too tight, acne-swollen face or missing teeth, a deep robot voice, another one edging towards hysteria. But it's not odd to me. I know that people come in two kinds, and one kind is broken. That's why they're here—to get fixed.

Frankie stumbles in, insulated in the heavy smell of cow shit. The teachers have begun to call Frankie by her full name, Francesca, encouraging her feminine side. They make her wear dresses, pull her dusty brown hair back in barrettes, but she still spends all her time with the manure spreader, she's in love with it. She sleeps with a pitchfork.

People begin gasping theatrically at her smell. One of the teachers gently tells Francesca she has to wash. The teacher leads her out.

I'm sitting right next to my mother, who is holding my little sister on her lap. Beky is just a doughy little bit with wispy blond hair, but she's already got hold of some power. My father calls her Bekah Blue, and she has his British accent. Blue is his favorite color, and she is my father's favorite. She owns that. Plus, when I tease her, she turns into a wild dog, biting and clawing, and I run crying to my mother. And Beky is a genius because she is only two and has already remarked in her stiff British accent, Tears are little bits of sadness.

My mother doesn't really play favorites, she makes everyone feel all right. But I am my mother's oldest daughter. My mother loves a conversation, and I am a good talker, better than my sister, who just makes her supposedly profound pronouncements and then twirls her hair and is silent. I am exceptionally, always, all right.

My mother stands now, holding my sister on her hip. She says calmly, Who called this meeting and why?

I stand up too, fold my arms over my chest. I did, I say. Someone wrecked my dollhouse.

General hilarity and excitement. Two students clap their hands out of sync.

I know who did it, I say.

Breath held, it's quiet now. I wonder if my dad is going to get pissed off over the destruction. If he does, there'll be hell to pay. I remember when a student named Maddy chased me down the stairs after I messed with her Barbie doll collection. My father punched her. I know other people remember this, too.

Billy did it, I say, narrowing my eyes at him.

Billy laughs nervously, like gagging. Billy has black hair that hangs in his eyes, his hands and legs are always on the move. He makes booby traps everywhere—spiderwebs of string in doorways that are supposed to trip you up. I like to show him how I can get through his booby traps, step right over or in between, he can't keep me out. He just gag laughs, says "booby trap" like he is deeply in love with the words and keeps looping his white string.

Once, while we were eating dinner, Billy had an epileptic seizure. Everyone crowded around. By the time I pushed my way through, it was all over. He had collapsed, strands of his black hair sticking to his wet face, his head resting on someone's arm. I wanted to ask where he went while he shook, maybe I did ask, but I don't remember the answer.

Now, my mother says, Billy, did you play with her dollhouse?

He booby-trapped it, I interrupt. And he has to say sorry. He has to get down on his knees and ask my forgiveness. I look to my father, but he's busy whispering in someone's ear.

My mother says, Billy, Micah seems very upset. She would like you to apologize.

Billy grins, says, Forgive me, your hiney.

People laugh. Thank you, Billy, my mother says. She pats my shoulder.

That's not good enough! I say. He has to get down on his knees.

Sharon, Billy's girlfriend, nervously volunteers to help with dollhouse repair. Sharon is always saying, Make nice. Sometimes Billy gets on the loudspeaker and broadcasts across the valley, Sharon is a sexy girl.

I shake my head. I'm not making nice.

Honey, my mother begins in her reasonable voice, but my father interrupts. Finally. I imagine my father commanding everyone to fall to their knees. My father had wanted to name me Boadicea, after his favorite pagan warrior queen, who led the Celts into battle against the Romans, screamed bloody incantations, then killed herself when she realized she had been vanquished. Although my mother refused to call me that, Boadicea is still my middle name, and all the awkward curtsies should be mine.

But my dad says, Billy, do you want to join the Royal Navy? *What?*

Billy laughs wildly.

My father will be the admiral; Billy can be a seaman, 3rd class. My father leaps from his tier of the amphitheater, goes to the closet, pulls out two large cardboard boxes. The return address is a costume supply company in New York. Everyone is speechless as my father unsheathes his knife, slices the boxes open and begins tossing out blue wool jackets with brass buttons, white breeches, black pointed shoes.

My mother says, But, Honey, we don't have a boat—

My father reveals another surprise. He has purchased two twenty-foot lifeboats, painted them red and yellow, outfitted them with cannons and sails—they are in harbor on Lake Champlain right now. He's ready to recolonize.

Billy, will you join?

Billy nods slowly. Right now.

Boys stand up, my father begins helping them into costumes, buttoning them up. He turns away Sharon. Sorry, long-standing tradition, no women in the Royal Navy.

All the boys are dressed. The women watch, I watch.

Onward, Maties! My father says.

Dad! I whine, what about me?

He pulls out two miniature coats. You and your sister are the home guard. He reveals that he has outfitted a miniature sailing boat and placed it in the field, just for us.

And my mother, she is thinking—I'm proud to tell you her IQ's off the charts, so the thoughts fly thick and fast—where did the money come from, how much of it, what about drownings, but the surprise of it, what the gesture says about our spontaneity, the glamour, the grandeur of the gesture, she doesn't want to be the kind of person who says, But.

My mother smiles at my father. All right. Have fun.

One of the other teachers says, What about reading group? We were in the middle of reading group.

My mother says, Don't worry. You can do reading group tomorrow. That's what this place is all about.

My father leads all us sailing men out the door.

Of course, I can't really go, I'm too little, I'm a girl (although Bekah Blue would surely go, if allowed). There are a million good reasons why I can't go out in a leaky lifeboat with ten costumed schizophrenic teenaged boys, all drunk on rum. Did I mention that no one knows how to sail, including my father?

But you go. Don't be afraid. It's fun. It's educational. It's like this. My father thinks Lake Champlain is too tame for the Royal Navy. You'll hitch up the boats to the bus and the pickup truck and head for Maine. You'll drive twelve hours, arrive at Penobscot Bay near midnight. You'll roll out a sleeping bag or wrap yourself in a blanket, sleep on the wharf or curled on a seat in the car or in the back of the pickup truck. In the morning, my father orders everyone to eat the traditional Royal Navy breakfast— onion sandwiches and rum.

The bay is grey and irritated. Climb on board, grab an oar, the admiral makes everything fun. Off you go to the middle of the bay, rowing for hours, blisters splitting your palms. My father chooses not to row, but he's the official keeper of the rum and the song leader. *Row you bully boys row.* You can hardly see the shore now. The tide is going one way, the wind another, the boat is listing. The admiral can't swim, but he wears a head-to-toe orange flotation suit under his officer's uniform.

How well can you swim? The bay is cold this time of year. But you can't get off now. Just swig some more rum, keep rowing, if you have to take a leak or throw up, feel free to do so over the side. Row. Sing, put your heart into it, boys, shout it, *John and Mary went to the dairy, John pulled out his big canary, way haul away, we'll haul away, Joe.*

Meanwhile, back at the ranch, what's happening?

I'm sailing over the green grass in my child-sized red and yellow ship with its real rudder and sail, in my real navy wool coat with brass buttons. I'm singing, *Mary said, Now that's a whopper, let's lay down and do it proper, way haul away, we'll haul away, Joe.*

And like my father, I am half-crazed with love for my mother. You should see her, with her long dark hair, her double-rowed smile, her bright red minidress with the lime green dots and her brown leather sandals with a small leather strap that goes over the big toe. She holds both her big toes slightly up and tensed, and the little leather straps tether them down.

She is my local deity. If I want to ascertain the truth from someone, I say, Swear to Mom? If my father is god of fire, god of laughter and seduction, god of fiction, then my mother is the creator, goddess of the anaerobic embrace, giver of succor, the one who cleaves.

With my father away and my mother in charge, these are placid times on Mount Olympus. The women are learning to read, they're in therapy groups, in morning meetings, they hike to a little waterfall and have a picnic beside it. There's a pajama party.

My mother has a little surprise for all of us who are left behind. She tells us to search the woods. I'm not sure what we're looking for, but I push through some bushes and my heart freezes. In a clearing, the sun pours down on a big tree with thick limbs. Lollipops and gumdrops grow from the branches.

Then one of the students finds the tree, she coos and begins picking. Everyone descends, laughing and eating, but for a while I just stand there, amazed at what my mother can coax into flower.

My father is home from his adventures in Maine, the returning hero. Or, at least he should be home. Everyone else has stumbled or swaggered in last evening, sunburned, blistered and hungover, but where is he, nobody seems willing to know. Don't worry though, my father always returns bearing gifts (and don't concern yourself with the money, the tuition keeps coming, and my mother will figure out the bills). There have been squirt guns for everyone in the valley, antique quilts and tricycles and dolls for us, a clutch of baby raccoons, fancy pigeons with fan tails, a team of workhorses. Once a baby goat for me, a brown one with a white muzzle. I named her Fern. I fed her sometimes. Another time a black-and-white pony. I named her Pepper. I ride sedately round and round the corral, wearing my red cowboy shirt and tasseled vest and ten-gallon hat he brought me from Frontier Town.

For my mother, my father brings tight maxi-length psychedelic dresses and those minidresses that graze her butt, antique necklaces, turquoise earrings.

You'll get your present, all you have to do is wait, but patience is not a family virtue. This particular night, alone, my mother has slept uneasily. Where is he? A car accident?

At sunrise she is woken by my father crowing, Good morning. She opens her eyes just as her arms are filled with knobby legs. My father has let fall a lanky spotted fawn. The fawn scrambles around on the bed, brown eyes rolling, dropping pellets, its miraculous, hard little hooves battering my mother so she cannot remember what to ask.

My father drops off the fawn in the tack room in the barn. It's a frosty October morning, he's home from his adventures, so we'll take the day off. My sister, my father and I line up on the cot in the office to get our hair done. My father likes his braided, but I don't want mine brushed or combed anymore. I stick it up in my wool beret. My mother says, You could fry an egg on your hair, it's that greasy, or It's so tangled it looks like a bird's nest, but she lets me go on stuffing it up in that hat. My sister's hair has slowly snarled until one side is eight inches shorter than the other, with a tangled knot the size of a real bird's nest over one ear.

Hair is warmth, freedom, an outpouring straight from the brain. The students who can, grow giant afros with picks tucked inside them; those with straight hair wear it long; boys and men sport wispy goatees or grizzly beards that run under their chins. People are free with their armpit and leg hair. Panda always has burrs in her long black fur. Even our cattle dress in shaggy, tangled coats.

I imagine all of us asleep in our beds on a cold autumn night, the dog snoring under the table, the cattle grunting in their stalls, all our hair beginning to grow, sliding silently over our pillows, slipping along the floor, out windows, through frozen fields, weaving orange cow hair with wiry pubic hair and children's corn silk, dog fur with men's bushy beards, a matted hair quilt blanketing the valley.

This morning, my mother runs her fingers through each head in turn, gently combing out the easier tangles, covering the matted hair over with the smooth. Then, she tries to dress, but we worry her, snapping her bra, pinching her butt. We cannot get enough of her—her pale breasts, her soothing, reddened hands, the perfection of her.

Stop, she says mildly, she never loses her temper. She finishes her own braid. Then we're off to leaf peep.

We like this fall game, because my father has his own way of seeing. He says, That one's gorgeous, lifting his chin towards a tree that, to the rest of us, looks dank and brown. When we drive through a whole tunnel of brilliant orange maples, he winces. Awful.

I squint, trying to make myself go color-blind.

When we grow bored of leaf peeping, the three of us beg and bully my mother into singing show tunes. As a little girl she went to musicals with her father. On the way home to Brooklyn in the car, they would belt out the score together, neither caring that my mother couldn't sing. But that was a kinder, gentler car.

In our Land Rover, with the first flat, nasal lyrics of the few songs she knows, "Old Man River" or *Oklahoma! Every night my honey Lem and I,...* we go hysterical, collapsing against each other, shrieking with laughter.

We have so much fun, it's just that sometimes my mother misplaces my father. She's done it again. He drove the two miles to pick up the mail, hours ago. It is close to midnight, early November, my mother sits on the cot in the office above the kitchen, thinking, Accident.

Have I mentioned how hard my mother works? It's all the time. The log cabin has not been built yet, so she even sleeps in the school office, we all do. She works until she gets sick, that's her break. My father's absence makes her feel exhausted now, as if a flu is coming on. Part of her wants to sleep, but she keeps imagining that accident. She watches insects crawling over the window, searching for a way in. The cot she is sitting on doubles as a couch by day, her and my father's bed at night. Beky and I are asleep under the Indian print bedspread on the cot we share head to toe, opposite the wall of filing cabinets and cluttered desks. There's one small window in the sloping attic roof, but now it just looks out on darkness.

My mother tiptoes down the narrow back stairs, out the communal kitchen door. The night is quiet, frost in the air. My mother cradles herself with her arms, feels her nose begin to run with the cold. Panda, our Newfoundland, plods by her side. She walks quickly down the drive, past the line of spruce trees that shield the house from the dirt road, thinking, What if the girls wake up alone? My mother sees our car parked by the barns. He's here, then, somewhere.

Bats glide in and out of the hayloft. She imagines that he has spent the evening trading with local antique dealers, bought something they cannot afford. He has begun to collect antique weaponry. He has flintlock rifles, crossbows, two cannons and a blunderbuss. Or maybe this time he bought a mule, an ostrich, who knows.

She walks up to the car. Behind the dust-smeared glass she sees movement. She taps on the window. My father and the young local girl they hired to help in the kitchen clamber out of the backseat. My father pats the girl's back, the girl looks at the ground. She is very upset, he explains. They were having a long talk. Her boyfriend is giving her trouble, my father has already promised she can spend the weekend.

It's true, she does look upset. My mother says she can stay here, sleep in the meeting room. They go back into the main house and my mother makes eggs and bacon for everyone, then calls the girl's parents to let them know everything is all right.

It is around this time that my mother begins to develop a form of migraine in which she goes temporarily blind.

It's winter now, it almost always is in the Adirondacks, from the first snowfall in October through the last hard frost in May. November, pine and spruce sag under their white burdens. By December, the snow on the ground rises higher than our heads, so we leave the main house through six-foot walls of packed snow. In memory, winter is dazzling white, with startling streaks of color. Red and blue down coats, yellow dog pee, the brief red thrill of a cardinal. The smell of wet wool on a heater, smells of mildew, steaming food and steaming breath of cows and humans and manure. Icicles ringing houses, hanging off people's noses and beards.

Late afternoon, snow tumbling outside, we're all in the main house living room. There's plastic stapled over the windows, and the woodstove melts the snow off the scarves and mittens clothespinned on the line above it. My mother's doing paperwork, my father's playing poker. I crouch under the table while my father deals. His fedora at a rakish angle, he sucks on his cigar in one corner of his mouth and tells jokes in his fake John Wayne accent out of the other. I watch the cards slip to the floor, his foot covering them. This does not surprise me. My father seems restless, though, tired of winning. He drops his cards on the table, pushes his chair back, stumps out his cigar. Let's go to the movies! he says. It's only an hour away through a snowstorm.

Everyone who wants to go bundles up in damp gloves and mittens and heavy winter boots. My mother leaves Beky and me with someone, they load up the van and off they go.

They return five hours later. The door bursts open and they sweep in on a rush of snow and cold wind. They're giddy, bumping up against each other. *Cool Hand Luke* has made them miss dinner. My mother says she is so famished, she could eat a pound of spaghetti. In the spirit of Paul Newman's egg-eating contest in the film, my father quickly turns my mother's hunger into a wager. He fills a metal mixing bowl with pasta. Everyone crowds round to watch my mother shovel it in, she who does not believe

in snacking, does not care for sweets, never varies from her 123-
pound weight.

My mother sits calm and undaunted before the pasta, as if she
expected a Rumpelstiltskin. My sister and I shove between hips
and elbows, trying to get the best seat, but we are crowded out
by the teenagers. I end up with a view that ends below her nose.
I watch as her fork rises and the first perfect swirl of spaghetti
enters her mouth. Another perfect swirl, another slow bite.
Another. She is full.

No contest. I laugh along with the general roar, vaguely disappointed, but mainly reassured that the world is a stable place,
its immutable laws intact.

Let's skip the rest of winter, in which nothing else happens, to
spring, the season of change. I like nice surprises, for example a
surprise gift is good, but I don't particularly like change. I like
enclosed worlds, stories inside their bindings, dollhouses, a cardboard box fort, the world inside the paperweight, the kaleido-
scope, the ballerina on top of my music box, the attic office room
where we sleep.

But stories feed on change, and now, we have one. My father
is building us a log cabin on the top of a hill behind the main
house. He hires a local shipbuilder, Blood and Sons. This does
not seem like a good sign. Ships tip, and then there's that name—
Blood.

There are bulldozers, cranes, giant logs, piles of slate and
sand, trees pulled over at crazy angles, the whole project is mon-

strous. My father asks me if I want my own room. I imagine a door thudding shut. Absolutely not.

To get away from the scraping, heaving noise and the dust, I go down to the creek. This is June, some of the students have left for the summer, but the blackflies are back, and the white-throated sparrow, too. I jump from rock to rock, making my way down the swollen creek. I follow as it winds into the woods. I find a rock with a flattish top. I sit there, on the grey rock in the middle of the water. I like the mumbling sound the current makes. The trees, new-leafed, baby green, crowd round me. I can't see or hear anyone. I do not feel like myself. I am like a child in a fairy tale, mysterious, alone.

From far off, I hear the meeting bell ring. Then my mother calls me, the way she always does, drawing out the end of my name like a long sigh. For some reason I remember a story she told me, about Persephone. Alone and away from her mother, she was pulled into the underworld. I am suddenly frantic to get home, as if I can feel Pluto's hand on my ankle. Instead of climbing back downstream I splash through the water and push through bushes. I'm surprised how close I am to civilization, just a few feet and there they all are, heading in their disorderly orderly way into the main house for a meeting.

Who called this meeting and why?

My father stands, one foot on the lowest green bench. He is holding his leather belt, and he keeps smacking it against his raised knee.

He says, Billy is dead.

No one speaks. I look over at Sharon. Her eyes are swollen and my mother is holding her hand. She already knows.

They believe a seizure came while he swam with his family on vacation.

I watch the knee that my father keeps hitting. The belt makes a snapping sound.

It was a reservoir, he says, and they drained it to find him.

I wonder if my father's knee hurts.

His parents want to bury him here, where he was happy and secure for the first time in his life.

When I look up from the knee, I see my father is crying.

Later, I watch my father carve Billy's name in stone. The carving takes all day, a hammer hit against a chisel, over and over, the noise of the chisel drowned out by the larger noise of the construction of our new home. I am jealous that Billy could make my father weep, that my father would spend hours working his name into a rock. (I bet he would do it for Bekah Blue.) But I don't want to have a seizure or turn into ash, and when my father looks up, his teeth clenched, I get spooked and run to my mother.

By late summer, the cabin is finally finished. My father and mother lead us up the hill. Downstairs is the kitchen-dining-living-parents' bed room. Upstairs is our sleeping loft. Instead of a banister, my father has knotted rope and hung it from ceiling to stairs, like rigging on a ship. My sister and I both want to be first up the stairs, we're pushing, elbowing. She makes it first. We begin to slap and pinch, and she goes into her feral beast routine. Mom, I scream. My mother calls up, exasperated, Just sit on her.

I'll give it a try. I rush at her, ram my head into her stomach, get her on the floor, drop my butt on her chest, hold down her arms. She's foaming at the mouth, but for the first time, I have her under my control. When I finally let her up, she's overcome with impotent fury, runs screaming down the stairs.

I can hear her telling on me.

I'm afraid of what my father will do, since I damaged his baby. I make the preemptive strike and yell down, I want my own room.

This irritates my father, after all the work Blood and Sons has done. He grabs hammer and saw; he hammers and saws for two frenzied hours. I stay out of his way. When he's done, he's walled my sister's bed off from mine, although it's just a wooden partition, five feet high.

But the labor seems to have gentled him, and after dinner, my father drinks rum and tells us stories of his childhood. My father is full of stories, especially about when he was a little boy in England.

Tonight, my father tells about the time he made a big mistake. He told his teacher at school about his dreams and visions that he considered to be as real as his everyday existence. They wanted to send him to a doctor, but his mother would have none of it. They tried to beat it out of him, but he just lied first, then said nothing. So they flunked him into a class called X. It was the English form system, A, B, C, etc.... He was in the X class for three years.

X was great, says my father. There were about eight of them in the class. All the other forms had twenty to thirty boys in them. In the English system boys were separated from girls at the age of eleven just to try and prevent them from becoming interested in any sexual games with the opposite sex. It meant you had sex with other boys or would have to find a way to tunnel into the girls' school. My father's gang in X did both.

Half the day they would have classes and the other half they would work in the garden or polish the floors or do something useful for the Romans: like make tea for the teachers. One day, my Dad's pal, Plug, pissed into the tea water to see if the dumb Romans would notice. They didn't. So they would all take turns until they got to Wally. Wally was part gypsy with really strong pee. So the teachers started to investigate the school water supply. It was getting too close to home so they stopped. My father knew the teachers thought he was dumb. It never occurred to the teachers what the boys in X thought of them.

Their teacher, Mr. James was okay. He was classified as a handicap himself, and this had kept him out of the army. He enjoyed them, and because they were crazy, they were allowed to laugh in class. In the other forms they had to sit in rows with their arms folded. They had to march everywhere in double columns. Just like you know who. The Romans.

But boys in the X class were a real tribe. They were all real Celts. Time and again they would get Mr. James to tell the tribal stories and myths. Boadicea was their Goddess. They built a shrine to her in the woods. They never worshipped God. He was male, and for young boys, all the tribal gods were women. They would paint themselves blue. Blue was their color. They would always wear something blue. Blue tie, blue socks, blue shirts, whatever. Crazy Harmon used to drink all the blue ink from the inkwells. He had some belief that it would turn his skin permanently blue. It did not. My father was surprised.

Once, the headmaster, a retired army officer, came to their class and was pleased that they were learning so much about history. He told them a story about how great the ancient Roman army was; that it brought law and order to Britain. They could not believe their ears. They sat in frozen silence. He must have thought they were enthralled because he went on for hours about Roman accomplishments. At the end he said, Boys, you are doing so well that you will soon be out of here and into regular forms.

That was it. They had an emergency meeting down at the end of the field.

We have to go underground, said Cassidy, the Irish boy. Just like the IRA.

No, no, said Plug, they're just a bunch of murderers.

They all looked at each other.

Why don't we just act more like ourselves? said Crazy Harmon.

That was it! They all turned to look with new admiration at Harmon. He had saved the tribe. Later, they lost him.

The woodworking teacher, who bullied everyone, hit Harmon about the head in a rage one day, and Harmon hit back. Other teachers came running in and they dragged Harmon off to the headmaster's room. X did not see him until the whole school assembled in the hall next morning, which they did every day to sing school songs and hymns and Roman anthems. The song they liked was Blake's, *And did his feet in ancient times*. Most of the words were tribal until the God part. After hymns would be announcements and then punishments, which could mean anything from having your name read out to being called in front of the whole school.

Two teachers marched in Harmon. There was a stool set up onstage. Harmon faced the school while the charges were read out. The X boys were in the front row. He looked at them. My father remembered the pain and anguish in his terrified eyes. Then an amazing thing happened. Seeing them, his heart brothers, Crazy Harmon winked. It was the bravery of a true pagan warrior, that wink. After that they dragged him over to the stool, took down his trousers and gave him twelve cuts of the cane. One for each fucking Apostle. Towards the end he sobbed uncontrollably. My father flinched at each stroke. Tears rolled down Plug's cheeks. They were choked in my father's throat.

Later on when my father was older he saw a movie called *The Loneliness of the Long Distance Runner*. He cried through the whole movie. He was crying for Crazy Harmon and the wink of bravery. They never saw Harmon after the caning but they heard he had been sent to another school on a training ship for boys. My father imagined him chained to the oars in a Roman galley.

After a long story like that, my father slugs rum, laughs, passes his hand over his mouth.

Now, it's time for bed; my mother tucks us into our new mattresses on the floor. After she goes down, I drag my pillow to Beky's room and climb in beside her.

I lie there and stare at the new ceiling, listen to my sister make her sucking noises (she's nostalgic for nursing). I think of all the stories I know. My mother doesn't remember her childhood, she seems to have arrived on the planet with breasts, ready for dating, but she has read to me about Laura Ingalls Wilder and Abraham Lincoln, they both grew up in log cabins, too. But it is my father as a child who is my constant companion.

When the war breaks out, my father's father tells him that war is like when two people get angry with each other. That is the only thing my father remembers his father ever saying to him.

My father keeps being evacuated during the war, but he causes trouble and is returned. At home, the front of their house has been torn off by a bomb. They have hung a long piece of canvas over the front, and the house is very dark. His family is busy with the war effort. His father joins the home guard. His mother drives an ambulance; she does abortions on their kitchen table, many for girls who've gotten in trouble with American soldiers. His mother burns the fetuses in the stove. She sews my father clothes from the shrouds from dead bodies. His older sisters date American sailors. Sometimes they bring their beaus home and have sex with them in the canvas-darkened room, in the same bed in which my father pretends to sleep.

My father is sometimes hungry, and tired of bread smeared with grease. My father is always scheming. He often goes out with a baby pram to steal coal. The pram looks innocent and works as well as a wheelbarrow. One night, he sneaks into a neighbor's back garden. He feels for the flowers with his hands, runs his palms down the petals, tries not to damage them. Then he pulls them up. In his haste, most of the flowers come up by the roots, hollyhocks, lupines, foxglove. He tries to pick roses but they cut his fingers. He takes what he has and flees, the flowers bent over on their long stalks, their hairy roots flailing, spraying dirt. He goes home, chops off the roots with his sheath knife. A Yank soldier gave him this knife when my father told him, Me dad's been killed by the Krauts. Early next morning, he takes the flowers to the train station, to sell. He uses the money to buy whale meat. He eats the whale with the Yank's knife.

As I fade into sleep, I imagine whale meat, the consistency of Jell-O, the taste of fingernails. I imagine the taste of ink in Crazy Harmon's mouth, sour and blue . . . I wake to the sound of hammering. At first I think my father is at it again, building walls. But then I realize a woodpecker has flown down the chimney and is now working on the beam above the bed. I cover my head with my hands and run downstairs to my parents' bed. I leap in next to my mother. Swearing, my father gets out, loads his twenty-two. He kills the woodpecker on the third shot. I hear the thud as it hits the floor. I'm glad it's dead, but I know we will probably have to eat it in a bony stew tomorrow night.

The next morning, Dad is plucking the woodpecker, Mom is talking on the phone while the toast burns, my sister is careful not to start anything with me. I look out the front windows that still have their new Agway stickers. I can see the whole valley from our hill. The Romans can never reach us here.

It's autumn 1968. Martin Luther King is assassinated, and then Bobby Kennedy is shot to death in the hotel kitchen. My father builds a complicated funeral pyre from all the guns in his collection. He pours gasoline on and burns everything.

I am almost five. My mother says I am going to go to school. My father says I don't have to if I don't want to. My mother says, Try it.

She waits with me in the grey morning by the barn. The chickens squabble amongst themselves. A bus trundles through the early morning fog. It stops and the door opens. I climb on. There is no one else on the bus but the driver. I choose one of the hard green seats, and the bus turns around in our driveway and starts back down the dirt road. We pick up our nearest neighbor's teenage daughter next.

This is a young woman I envy. My mother and I visited once, and I was allowed to walk across the field to inspect her old playhouse. The pristine playhouse had a linoleum floor, Formica table, gingham curtains. Its perfection awed me, and I sat at the little table in silence.

Mom has asked this teenager to sit with me on the bus. She does, and we are alone, watching trees, for a long time. But then there are more houses, and her friend gets on and squishes into the seat. They both have big girl butts that press me against the wall. They talk and talk and the bus fills up with kids, screaming and calling to each other. I look out the window, thinking, I will be quiet and I will not be caned.

My teacher's name is Mrs. Windle. The boys have crew cuts and striped shirts. The girls wear plaid jumpers and black shoes. I've seen kids like these before in the Dick and Jane books they use in reading group at the valley school, but it never occurred to me Dick and Jane were real.

It's hard to tell kids apart. The desks are all the same, too. At nap time I put my mat by the teacher's desk and lay there in the dim room, not sleeping. My mother bought this rug specially at Newberry's and it doesn't smell like home. At show-and-tell a girl shows a toy that makes animal sounds. A mechanical pig's grunt. A chicken's squawk. Two kids try to hold hands, but the teacher says, Hands to yourself. We cut and glue and paste and color.

The next morning there is school again. This is exhausting. I thought it was a onetime thing. My father says, You don't have to go. My mother says, Try it, and walks me down to the bus. Every morning the same thing.

My father runs a snapping turtle over in the car, brings it home for turtle soup. He shows me how the turtle heart keeps beating, a pulsing grey teardrop, all by itself on the butcher block, never realizing it is alone. He cleans out the enormous shell and gives it to me for show-and-tell. But I am too shy. The teacher shows it for me. The outside of the shell is covered in faint grey and green patterns. The inside is ridged, like mountains. I hold onto the turtle shell for the rest of the day.

The teacher asks a girl named Faith to walk beside me to the playground. She has curly brown hair and missing front teeth. I'm not sure if I have a conversation with her, but she comforts me. I think we hold hands in the playground.

One afternoon coming home on the bus the teenaged neighbor girl is not there to wall me in. Two boys from kindergarten class sit beside me. Why don't you ever talk? they ask.

I stare straight ahead.

Talk, they say.

I won't.

They hit me. Talk, they chant, getting a rhythm going, Talk, drumming on my shoulders and chest and back, Talk. If you just talk, we'll stop hitting you, one boy says, sounding tired.

I am brave, like Crazy Harmon, because my father is watching. I cry, but just tears, no sound.

A few days later, Faith is absent from school. I start to cry, in the middle of cutting and pasting. I hold my middle so Mrs. Windle thinks I have a stomachache. She asks one of the other girls to walk me to the nurse. The nurse lays me on a cot behind a curtain and leaves the office. I begin to wail. The nurse's heels click down the hall towards me. She yanks back the curtain, I could hear you from all the way at the principal's office. Be quiet, she hisses. But I keep it up.

Then my father is there. I can tell he's not mad at me, he thinks I did the right thing. On the way out, he lifts me up to take my first drink from a water fountain. When we get home, my mother is not mad either, because she says I gave it a try. I never go back to kindergarten.

On my fifth birthday, Faith appears in a party dress, with a present. This seems entirely out of place. I don't say much to her, just show her the barn and the cows. I'm relieved when she does not return.

A few weeks later my mother receives my report card. We are graded with either a smile face or a frown face. In the box for Social Skills, there are no faces. Mrs. Windle writes that I did not speak once in six weeks.

CHAPTER THREE

warrior bride

1969–1970

IN KINDERGARTEN last year, the Romans beat me and cut out my tongue, but I escaped, and toughened. My mother buys bags of chicken hearts from the butcher at the Grand Union in town. I stand by her hip while she fries them in butter in the iron skillet, then I chomp the little organs one by one. I have a passion for the soft, dry cookies called Lady's Fingers. The sound of the plastic ripping off, the way the pale pink fingers nestle against each other. I rip a finger off, stuff it in my mouth, rip another, eat two hands' worth.

You'll see. Today, a day in September, two months after Buzz Aldrin and Neil Armstrong put a three-by-five-foot metallic American flag on the moon, I come upon my father working beneath our own row of flags. He crouches on a giant circle of canvas, biting his lower lip with his Stonehenge teeth, painting green stripes and blue circles. I study the painting. I bite my lip with my own newly jumbled front teeth. I ask my father what he's doing. He says it is a teepee—he has decided to form an Indian Warrior Society. He says everyone can join, even the children. I take off to spread the news.

Bo is the first person I want to tell. The school has expanded. There are now thirteen staff members' children. We have our own two-room school at the far edge of the valley. I wear my striped wool tam every day, my hair stuffed up into it. My sister likes to wear her pajamas morning to night. In these outfits, we stop for Bo and his brother at their trailer and head up to the Little School each morning. There, we play cards, read, draw, are read to, try out some algebra, some Spanish, and play Barbies and GI Joes.

Bo is the perfect best friend. He has black hair that his mother saws off at his shoulders and just above his green eyes; his smile is wicked. His father was an Olympic skier, and Bo already has the physical confidence of an athlete. He is heroically disposed: at seven, he pulls nails from our feet and drives his mother's VW up and down the dirt road. He has enthusiasm for all games of pretend. He's sneaky, mean, kind and daring.

Now, I find Bo and his little brother, Dustin, about to let the pigs out of the pen. This is a favorite activity. We drag open the gate and the pigs jostle each other onto the dirt road. The meeting bell rings, the whole school chases after the pigs as they crash around the fields, squealing. We sit on the roof of a truck, munching penny candy if we have it, and watch the action.

But now, before Bo begins to pull on the gate, I say, Forget the pigs. We're moving to that hill up there. Everybody, the whole school. We're going to be warriors.

I'll get my gun and meet you in front of the barns, Bo shouts, and he's off, his brother racing him to their trailer.

It never occurs to me that this world is alien to Bo. He doesn't mention that before this fall, he led a normal life in a split-level in Bozeman, Montana, where his housewife mom made him a lunch in a brown paper bag and he got on the school bus and drank milk from a small carton at his desk; after school, he got off the bus and his mom made him a snack and he went out to play. The next day was the same. But his parents have divorced, and his father is still in Montana, and their home has become a trailer pushed up against the woods at a hippie commune school.

Ellen, his mother, knew my mother from summer camp. She's our teacher at the Little School. Ellen has a Jackie O hairdo and is the only grown-up at the school who wears makeup. In warm weather she walks around in a bikini she crocheted herself. She puts ads in the personals for rich boyfriends. To get here, she loaded up her two boys and drove cross-country, wearing that crocheted bathing suit with a pistol stuck in the waistband.

When it's time to begin our lives as warriors, the whole school gathers in front of the barn carrying blankets, except my father, who has a buffalo robe slung over his shoulder. There are eight teachers, twenty disturbed adolescents and the thirteen of us.

We straggle up the dirt road edged in black-eyed Susans and daisies, through a hay field, then climb a hill at the edge of the valley. Most of us loiter around while Dad and the guys chop down trees and strip them to make teepee poles. We watch the new students and the old ones we know, lounging, smoking ciga-rettes, making wisecracks out of the sides of their mouths. The students are no longer just schizophrenic. We're at the point now where most are troubled teenagers referred by the courts. There is a sometimes uneasy mix of mental illness and bad attitude. To the kids with schizophrenia, and to us, the juvenile delinquents are as jaded and glamorous as movie stars.

There's Doug, my father's right-hand man. He has dark, wavy hair and a pretty smile. He laughs, it's an alcoholic Santa Claus chuckle, the kind of laugh that makes you want to be in on the joke. His hobby is duct-taping firecrackers to frogs, then watching them hop and explode. Angie, Doug's girlfriend, has long blond hair and an Arabian horse she brought from home. Angie was raped by two men when she ran away cross-country.

Wild, rangy, his face pitted with acne scars, Giovanni saw his uncle shoot his father in his own driveway. Giovanni plays chas-ing games with us for hours. He once got in trouble for sticking utensils up a dog's ass.

The teepees are almost done. Doug shimmies up a pole to cinch the top of each teepee. Doug has no shirt on, his tanned arm muscles swell and his jeans slide down over his slim hips. I want to marry him, I want to be just like him, but then Ann smirks, nudges Kitty, says something about Doug's skinny white ass. Kitty starts giggling.

I admire Ann's huge light brown afro with a white leather cap perched on top and the glittery pick in her back pocket, but Kitty is my hero. She wears her own hair in a short, perfectly groomed afro. She has deep brown skin, a body that seems smoothly rounded and hard at the same time. Picture her with a gold chain around her neck, a red, silky acrylic shirt that ends at her midriff, bell-bottom jeans, pick in her back pocket. Kitty is always throwing a fit, pulling someone's hair out and stalking off down the road. Everyone is afraid of her. She's perfect.

Skinny white ass, I scoff now, pawing the grass with my foot, pretending to put out a cigarette. Kitty laughs even more.

Doug jumps down. The teepees look pretty, up against the high, thin blue sky and the hills just beginning to burn red and gold.

My father lines up all the children. He gives us the once-over. He takes Bo's twenty-two, checks it out, uncocks it, looks down the barrel. Then he hands it to Doug. I see Bo's face working to keep the tears back. It's the gun his dad gave him, but Bo is scared of my dad, like everyone else, and he doesn't say anything.

My dad tells us we will be living off the land from now on. No store-bought food allowed. He gives a sheathed knife to each child. Hunt for your supper, he says.

My father begins passing out guns and knives to the juvenile delinquents.

We spread out through the woods, searching for small animals to kill. The forest is desultory, moldy leaves everywhichway, young saplings leaning on each other for support. The squirrels are too fast for us, even the newts and frogs are in hiding. Soon, we give up on meat and turn to berry picking.

On our way down to the blackberry bushes, just as we're crossing the road, a station wagon crawls towards us. Windows rolled up, the two young boys sport their back-to-school brush cuts, the mother in a kerchief, the dad with a cigarette. We stop by the edge of the road to let them pass. This is a common occurrence, sightseers driving past the funny farm for entertainment. I think I recognize one of the boys from my kindergarten days. I give the car the finger. Bo, Beky and the others follow suit. We head off across the next field, back to business.

We take shards of grey slate, left over from building the roof of our log cabin, and heave them onto the brambles. They settle, making tunnels into the prickers. We crawl in, but the blackberries are shriveled and taste of mold. Still, we sit in our thorny caves. We sing, "She'll Be Coming Round the Mountain When She Comes" and "All We Are Saying, Is Give Peace a Chance." When we grow hungry, we suck on white clover. Then we chase each other in and out of the teepees in the last of the cool September light.

At dusk, Dad calls Bo over. He slings an arm around him. I have a job for you, me boy. He leads him off to where the new male students are being initiated. I follow, at a distance. Dad, Brad and Doug have gathered the new teenagers by the stream. They're stripped to their skivvies. The new boys stand in a ragged line—drug addicts, runaways, truants and thieves. Skinny boys with shaggy hair, goose-pimpled arms crossed over ribs, smirking nervously. My father hands Bo a small shovel and gestures towards a bucket of cow manure. Dump it over their heads.

There's snorting and howling laughter, but none of them protest. Bo is smiling. Then, my father dips his own hand into the bucket, spreads his fingers and presses his hand against each chest. Now every boy has my father's handprint in shit over their hearts. Next, they leap into the frigid stream, the boys holding their hands over their dicks to guard against snapping turtles. They are warriors.

I don't know what the girls are, or where they are. Maybe with my mother, sitting in a circle, talking about their feelings. Wherever they are, they're not putting on as good a show.

For dinner there are blue jays and squirrels, skewered on sticks and grilled over an open fire. Dad has made this dish for my sister and me at home. My father chooses food primarily for its novelty. Our cupboards are filled with army rations in dull green tins. He cooks up steaming platters of cabbagy, wilting food he assures us is Chinese, or yellow curries he says he learned from his father, who'd learned how to make curry when he was a soldier in India. (My father lived with his father only until he was four, and I can't see the retired soldier trading recipes with a toddler, but these curries are part of the heritage my father invents for himself.)

When we refuse to eat the broiled blue jays he serves us at the log cabin, my father grows indignant and more British. This is a delicacy, he says, his fancy accent increasing. You girls would pay a fortune for this dish in any exclusive restaurant, it is called pheasant under glass. To prove it to us he brings us each our scrawny bird hidden under a cereal bowl. When that doesn't work, his accent turns working-class: When I was a boy, me mum served bread and drippings, and glad we was to have it.

In our new warrior life no one coaxes us to eat. There isn't enough stringy bird meat to go round. We are really hungry now. My mother makes fry bread. We all gather round, watching her cook the soft, oily bread in a cast-iron skillet over the fire. She begins to lift it off. The heavy pan tips. The bread slips into the ashes. There is a wild scramble as we all grab for the bannock, tearing it out of each other's hands. I hold my piece of blackened bread close to my chest. I remember the satisfying taste of soot and grease.

My father and mother begin to argue about whether she should go down to the main house to bring up extra provisions. My mother thinks, Yes, definitely—nourishment is her first priority. My father thinks, Absolutely not, the play is the thing. Both their voices grow huffy with irritation. Finally, my mother sighs. My father wins, and we go to bed hungry.

The night grows cold. Inside the teepees, we roll ourselves in blankets on the hard ground. In another teepee, we hear Dustin, Bo's little brother, crying from cold. My father takes him into his buffalo robe.

In our teepee, snuggled up against my mother, I imagine all the long days and nights of warrior life ahead of me, crouched on the ground, gnawing the skinny bones of squirrels. I imagine turning more and more wolfish, slinking through the forest with an empty stomach and sharpened teeth. I will be as tough as the students; hiss, Skinny white ass, as I bring down a deer with my bare hands.

That night, while we slept in our teepees, the Algonquins, people of the longhouse, may have walked softly out of the woods to investigate. So, too, the mulish nineteenth-century farmers. The Swedish iron miners hike down from their ghost town on the ridge. They all want a glimpse of the future.

You can see the old moon, small and grey, but not the moon's metallic flag. They circle the teepees, the Algonquins in deerskin breeches and tunics, their heads shaved except for a topknot, the miners and farmers in cambric and wool. A miner lifts the flap of the teepee door, and they all peer in at the snarled heads of hair poking out of army blankets. Perhaps if I had woken then I would have seen them.

They drop the flap, shake their heads, click their tongues. An Algonquin man takes a stick and stirs the ashes of the fire, nudges out a blue jay skull. Everyone looks. They stare at each other. A farmer shakes his head. Progress, he says. They begin to grin and chuckle, then double over, slap each other on the back. They laugh so hard they disappear.

At dawn, we throw off our frost-covered blankets and duck out the teepee door. Dustin has peed all over my father's buffalo robe. Everyone is famished and whining. We gather up our blankets and march down Teepee Hill for breakfast. Living off the land has come to an end.

It's winter again in the Adirondacks, it almost always is. My father has directed the making of a toboggan course that starts on top of the ridge and barrels across our driveway all the way to the stream. Then, my father organizes Olympic trials. Everyone divides into teams. Dad has a stopwatch and a walkie-talkie and waits at the bottom of the hill in his huge red down jacket, while Les stands at the top with his own stopwatch and walkie-talkie and huge green down jacket. Les has arrived at the school in time for the Indian Warrior Society. He's brought his wife and his son, Toby, same age as me. He's a tall man with brown hair that he wears almost shaved, a little goatee and glasses that have a green tint to them. He, like my father, is an artist, a comic, a man that's been in trouble in school for mouthing off.

The teams crowd four to a toboggan, their jeans already stiff and frozen. The last person shoves off, jumps on and then everyone yells as the toboggan schusses down the slope. There are amazing wipeouts, people coming up covered in snow and blood, laughing. My father keeps track of the times, and Doug's team wins the winter Olympics. Les contests, says it was rigged. My father just laughs and hands Doug the medal.

That's the only thing that happened that winter. We spent most of it inside, dopey from heat, all the windows covered over with plastic for insulation. At school, Ellen read to us for hours, sometimes the whole day. We lounged on the window seats, heavy-lidded and warm, dreaming of Narnia where it is always winter or of the fierce snowstorms on the prairies when Laura Ingalls Wilder was a girl. We played cards, we played GI Joes and Barbies. Outside, there was frozen dog and cow and horse shit and bare trees.

Let's move on to June, when my parents' future lovers arrive. Paul and Laurie. They've come for an interview. The job openings are for a reading teacher and a farm manager, and both staff members will also be house parents. They will live in a dome attached to an A-frame that houses seven emotionally disturbed, mixed-sex students. The jobs are twenty-four hours a day, six days a week. Seven thousand a year, combined salary.

Paul is twenty-four, handsome as a Kennedy, dark wavy hair, dark skin, wide shoulders, son of a farmer, former college track star and class president, squeezed into a tweed jacket and tie; Laurie, former prom queen, wears an empire-waisted, green velveteen dress; both Paul and Laurie have large, very white teeth. They drive down in their red VW bug from the small college near the Canadian border where Paul is teaching Marxist sociology and Laurie is studying experimental education.

Why would they want to work here?

Because this is where it's happening, they say. This is practice, not theory.

My parents are skeptical. Paul and Laurie are so young, twenty-four, and they seem too straight. A lot of theory, no practice. My father plays King Arthur, gives them a quest. He hands over Giovanni and Maddy, asks Paul and Laurie to take them camping for two weeks. They agree. They drive off down the road with tents and sleeping bags roped to the top of their bug, Giovanni hunched over in the backseat next to Maddy who is clutching her Barbie doll case with one hand and pushing up her black plastic cat-eye glasses with the other.

They drive back down the road two weeks later. Everyone is alive and well. Paul is no longer in a suit, he's wearing jeans and a T-shirt and he's bearded now. Laurie wears a kerchief, blue corduroys and a smock shirt.

Giovanni sits on the main house porch with his friends, smokes a cigarette to drive away the blackflies. He's wearing overalls, no shirt. He says it was groovy. Maddy goes up to the log cabin and takes one of my father's guns along with some shells. She goes down to the bunker where Les and his family live. She waves the gun around, says she's going to kill the whole family. My mother, my father and Paul walk into the bunker. They disarm Maddy. There's a meeting to decide what to do next.

While all the adults are talking in the bunker, I come upon Bo crouched between the barns and the stream, building a Styrofoam boat. It's canoe-shaped, small and tidy. We gather up the others and plan an expedition: cross the swollen stream and explore the field that lies beyond it. The sun is warm, the wind cool and damp. Liquid green, that field is full of possibility, a land we've never been to.

The stream is below a steep embankment, most of it hidden from the road, but there is an old ladder down to it. Bo and I carry the boat above our heads, the rest dance around us as we climb down to the edge of the creek freed from ice a few months before. The boat is only big enough for Bo and one passenger, but he has a paddle, and battling the current, he ferries us over one at a time. Last is Les's son, Toby. Bo steps out of his craft where we are gathered on the far bank, paddle in hand, but before Toby can climb out, the current takes the boat. Toby stands in the canoe as it swirls down the stream. Hey, he says. He raises his hand to us, maybe to signal for help, maybe in farewell. We wave back. He disappears around a bend, and we forget him.

This distant shore, now that we are here, is not so appealing. It is bright green because it is a marsh, and we are up to our ankles in cold muddy water. Toby is always messing us up. Without the canoe, how will we return?

We rush along the shoreline until Bo finds a log angled over a narrower part of the stream. The log is steep, higher at one end than the other, rotten, slick with algae. Bo goes first, then me. Then my little sister, Beky. Except Beky slips. She still holds on to the slippery log with one arm, but the current is strong, and the water is freezing and over her head.

I turn once and see my sister's pinched face, her long hair swirling in the water, then I run for help. I sprint up the hill, my feet drumming the road, my hands in fists, my heart shouting, Danger.

Back at the stream, my sister's wool sweater is heavy with water, her rubber boots are filling. The stream is pulling at her so intently. She can't swim, but she thinks, Maybe I should just let go. And then she opens her hands and drops off the log. (In her memory, this is the defining moment of her childhood—she does not save herself.)

I fling open the door of the bunker. I can see all the important grown-up legs around the table. I am daunted for a moment, but the drama of the day is upon me. I yell, Beky's drowning!

The words are a miracle. The legs bolt to their feet, chairs are knocked over. They stampede past me and out the door.

Bo is a few feet below the log. He sees Beky tumbling towards him in the current. He wades in and grabs her sweater, hauls her out. Beky's choke-hollering. He looks around, it's just him and her. (This is Bo's crystallizing moment—grown-ups will not save you.)

By the time the adults skid down the embankment, Beky is not even crying anymore. My mother holds my bedraggled sister against her chest. Toby arrives, wet and outraged. He says the canoe is gone.

I want to race back and forth in the space between the danger and the rescue, the perpetual carrier of vital information. I feel a little crestfallen, had hoped at least for a more thrilling finish, a lasso maybe, a fire truck.

Maddy is gone, my father's guns are now locked in a closet and Paul's next trial is the haying. Late summer, early fall, the height of hay season. After the fields are cut and dried, they bring out the old thresher, a line of whirling disks with bent rusty spikes on the end. My father has painted them over in red and yellow flowers. When the thresher is parked, we stand between the disks and spin them, watching the colors and the nasty hooks blur within inches of us.

After the hay is bailed, my mother drives the tractor that pulls the wagon. The tractor trundles slowly over the fields while people grab the twine with their gloved hands and swing the bales up onto the wagon. It is always hot, everyone's backs are itchy with sweat and hay, everyone is happy (Bo can lift a hay bale all by himself). We clamber all over, sitting on the bales, leaping off the wagon and running beside. Later, we ride the green conveyor belt that takes the bales up into the loft.

The barn's loft is filled with hay and drifting feathers. Swallows swoop in the eaves above us. Light falls from cracks in the roof and lies on the hay like silk scarves. We burrow into the straw, play hide-and-seek. Bo and I always hide together, our arms wrapped around our legs, our heads on our knees, our shoulders touching, our breath loud in each other's ears. When we're found, we fling ourselves out of the loft onto a pile of loose hay on the ground.

This August, we're doing the usual, standing on the thresher, watching the disks whirl, the flowers and hooks blur, when someone says, Hey, you kids, get off there.

It's Paul.

We jump down. What?

You can't do that, he says. It's dangerous.

We've done it before, I say, cutting my eyes at him.

You could get hurt, he says. Play somewhere else.

This new guy is an asshole, I say. Bo and Beky agree.

Under Paul's supervision, it's the first haying season in which none of the machinery is broken. He's officially the farm manager, but I don't like the way he manages the farm. He makes up safety rules. I like rules, as long as they're mine. My rules keep me safe, my order is my own power, backed up by my father.

But Paul is my father's new right-hand man. Paul's hair is now long enough to wear in a beribboned ponytail, like my father. They go hunting together. He takes to wearing a fringed leather jacket and a leather hat, everyone calls him Adirondack Paul.

My mother has decided Paul is genuine, an intellectual farmer. He seems constitutionally incapable of telling a lie. She likes the way he rolls his cigarettes in the sleeve of his white T-shirt, the way he hums Bob Dylan's "Copper Kettle" as he fixes the split-rail fence by the horse barn or discusses Buckminster Fuller's theories of group dynamics. He reminds her of her girlhood hero, Abraham Lincoln.

Les is the one who finally told her, and this is how I imagine it happening. My mother is in the kitchen of the main house. She's doing dishes, or she's making matzoh ball soup. Everyone else is at some evening activity, maybe off at a movie in Glens Falls. Les comes into the kitchen and leans on the counter, his arms folded. He and my mother are easy together, they're friends from high school. He still calls her Tush Mgooch because in high school she had a big butt, even though since she's had children her butt has flattened.

I imagine my mother goes to the pantry to choose a spice. He stands just inside the doorway. There are shelves crowded with herbs and cans and mouse droppings. There's hardly room for both of them.

Les says, Tush, what's your arrangement with your husband?

What do you mean? She's on tiptoe, reaching for the top shelf.

Is it an open marriage or what?

She's got the oregano, turns to face him. No, it's not an open marriage.

But, you know, right? That he's sleeping around.

What are you talking about? My mother has an intense feeling of claustrophobia. She thinks she might faint, it's so hot and close in there. She pulls on the string, the bare bulb goes out, she pushes past Les, out of the pantry.

He follows her over to the stove. You need to know, everyone else does. Les is almost whispering now, I'm talking students, staff, the checker at the Grand Union, everybody.

My mother puts down the oregano and places her hand over her mouth. She wants to deny it, but how can she? Her careful collusion in her own deception is no longer possible. Now that it's been said she realizes she can name the times, starting with that girl in the back of the Land Rover, each unexplained disappearance, missed plane, broken car, each ridiculous excuse.

How is she going to make this all right?

I could say she turns the burner on high, lets the huge pot of soup boil over so that chicken soup cascades in a riotous river that drowns the damned. Or, she slaps Les hard, just because he's the messenger. But this would be out of character. Really, my mother would have taken her hand off her mouth, and she would have cried.

Later that night, she confronts my father in the log cabin. He grows indignant, denies everything. But she cites women and times. She says, You have to stop.

He's pacing now. Look, it doesn't mean anything.

Will you stop?

I'm not going to lie and say I'll stop. But it doesn't mean anything. Monogamy is bullshit, man. You should try making love with other people, too.

When my mother tells the story now, she says, We had open marriages in the valley for a very short period. We were trying to form the perfect community, without possessiveness, but it was always done with the understanding that everyone had a primary relationship, and the sharing would not threaten that primary relationship.

Sweetheart, you're the one I love, you're the love of my life, my father says. She believes him, he believes himself, I believe, too. Now everything is out in the open, things will only get better.

Marriage is a bourgeois institution, monogamy is suffocating, but weddings are rituals, weddings are fun. That September, Brad and his girlfriend nearly die on their own wedding day.

Brad looks like all the other male teachers. He has granny glasses, long hair and a mustache. I get all of those nice guys with long hair and mustaches mixed up: one twirled me around and sang "Taga, Taga"; one played the guitar for us; one crouched on the ground with us and explained the secret life of ants. Brad I remember because he was a special friend of my father's. They were always joking, messing around—they'd bend over, rub their hands together and cackle, play villains from a melodrama.

For the wedding, Brad's girlfriend wears a long muslin dress with embroidery and a gauzy veil. She is very pregnant. Brad wears a suit and no shoes. One of the other teachers marries them. Beky and I get to be the flower girls, carrying daisies and wearing red and blue paisley dresses. It is a beautiful fall day, wind whipping, green grass and blue skies.

Behind where they are performing the ceremony stands Billy's grave, the three-foot-high pile of grey stones with the plaque my father carved on top. That shimmer in the air could be Billy's ghost seizing, or he may just perch on his gravestones, calling, Sharon is a sexy girl.

At the end of the ceremony, the couple climb into an antique carriage led by a stamping black horse. My father and nine students, all dressed in eighteenth-century Royal Navy uniforms, raise their muskets and fire off a ten-gun salute.

The guns make a terrific noise, the horse whinnies, rears and gallops down the steep hill, dragging the carriage behind it. Everyone screams, choking on smoke and the acrid smell of gunpowder. Frankie, the student who spends all her time at the barn, runs in front of the carriage to stop them. The horse veers, Frankie falls and we all watch as a huge carriage wheel runs over Frankie's chest. Amazingly, like Wile E. Coyote, Frankie pops up and speeds after the runaways, waving her arms.

The horse and carriage are careening towards a stream at the bottom of the very steep hill, sometimes with one wheel off the ground, sometimes the other. The bride stands and begins pulling tight on the reins, just like Charlton Heston in *Ben Hur*, only pregnant. Her veil flies out behind her. Brad stands, too, holding her steady.

I glance at my mother's mouth, an O of horror, hand moving to cover it. Just as it occurs to me that this might be something more than spectacle, the horse and carriage stalls safely in the stream. The groom climbs out barefoot and carries his heavy bride through the freezing water. We cheer.

Afterwards there's a party in one of the domes. Black lights and fluorescent posters. A punch bowl full of grape juice and beer. Kitty stands up in a red minidress and thin white scarf draped grandly around her neck, huge silver hoop earrings. She sings "Swing Low, Sweet Chariot," and she sings "Rolling on the River." There are no tremors, only the good, strong voice filling the round room.

Then Kitty puts the Jackson Five on the stereo, *One Two Three, Baby You and Me, Girl.* Everyone dances. Doug asks me to dance. He's whirling me around, dizzying me. He yells over the music, When you're eighteen, I'm going to ask you out on a date.

Bo won't dance. He sits on a bench, head on his knees, he's often like this when the students are around. My sister is dancing with Ann, mimicking the way she shakes her legs. I go over to watch Kitty carefully put her record back in its jacket. She shows me the Jackson Five album cover, points out Michael, says, Since we're the same age, I could marry him if I want.

Someone else puts on the Beatles—*Come together, right now, over me.* Angie and Doug are making out on the couch. My father is dancing with Laurie, I hear him say he loves her fine cat eyes. And there are my mother and Paul, they're dancing so close, Paul moves like Elvis, my mother sways her hips from side to side. Maybe Billy is still here too, looping tangles of string around us all.

I am seven years old, drunk on grape juice and beer punch. The stereo croons, *What the world needs now, is love sweet love, it's the only thing that there's just too little of.* I am full of admiration for the gallant groom and his daring pregnant bride, for Frankie's cartoonish invincibility, for my father's genius for creating excitement. When I am eighteen, I will marry Doug or Michael Jackson on Ceremony Hill, and I will unflinchingly hold the reins while our horse gallops straight towards the worst danger.

Meanwhile, two hundred and forty miles away, in a suburban basement in Syracuse, the future husband is an eleven-year-old boy. He kneels on the floor, perfecting his model rocket. He pulls his T-shirt down over his embarrassingly big butt. He wears a ski hat to squash his curly hair flat. Beside him, a half-eaten blueberry Pop-Tart on a napkin and a glass of milk. He's a meticulous, ordered boy. His rocket looks exactly like the photograph on the package. For each drink of milk he takes a bite of Pop-Tart. The AM radio station is on low, playing last year's hits. He doesn't realize he's mumbling under his breath, along with Diana Ross, *Someday, we'll be together,* drawing out the last two syllables until his voice breaks. He reaches for the Pop-Tart, then the glass of milk, making sure everything comes out even.

CHAPTER FOUR

inuit adventure

Summer 1971

KINDERGARTEN is really all I know of the outside world so far, but my horizons are about to be expanded. My parents tell me we are going sailing in the Virgin Islands for our summer vacation. We will spend a month on a yacht with a captain and his first mate. This vacation idea scares me—Dad has read me *Treasure Island*, and I imagine the sailors as wooden-legged and treacherous. Then, my father says maybe instead we should go live with the Eskimos. He asks for my opinion. Definitely the Eskimos, I say, voting against the pirates.

It's settled, then. You see, on one of the Royal Navy adventures my father has met a renegade French Canadian priest who has done missionary work in the Canadian Arctic. This priest will arrange everything for us.

But that night I overhear my mother worrying. The Eskimos keep sled dogs, and in the summer they run wild, they've killed children. Now, I am not looking forward to this vacation either. My father writes a letter to the priest, and receives a letter back, saying that we can live with the town garbageman. The letter also reports that the dogs are now kept on a nearby island in the summer, no need to fear.

August. Bo and Dustin are off to Montana to be with their father, the students return to their fucked-up home lives for vacation. Paul and Laurie are on a camping trip. And we're going to the Canadian Arctic to live with the town garbageman for a month.

We drive to Montreal in our Land Rover. Then we take a plane to Timmins. At Timmins, the Canadian authorities confiscate my father's hunting rifles. Dad throws a fit, shouts at the bland customs officials, This is un-American! We're leaving this godforsaken country and going home. My mother soothes him, reminds him he still has all his new, expensive fishing gear.

My father condescends to remain in Canada. From Timmins, we board a World War Two seaplane and trundle off for Povungatuk on the Hudson Bay. There is a huge roaring in the cabin, and we have to yell to hear each other. The pilot leaves his door open so we can watch him fly the plane. It begins to rain, and water leaks onto our seats. We are given towels to hold against the roof. From the little window I see that the world has become half grey water and half dark green tundra, forever.

Finally, the plane begins to turn and descend. I see a straggle of pastel-colored shacks. Then we land in the ocean. The plane rocks. The pilot cuts the engine and heaves open the door. Waves splash his feet. We are about a hundred yards from shore. Four canoes make their way towards us, paddled by dark-haired men in parkas. A canoe pulls up alongside the door to the plane. The pilot lifts my sister and I onto the floor of the boat, and the men paddle away. I grip the gunnel as we splash through the waves. The men are talking and laughing in a language I can't understand. Mutiny, I think. My sister is silent, so the whimpering must be coming from me. When we near the shore, the man in the bow jumps into the frigid, knee-deep water and drives the canoe onto the pebble beach. A crowd of people circle us, all of them with dark, straight hair. They watch my sister and me as we are heaved out of the boat by our armpits. My mother and father and our luggage arrive. We all stand there.

Then the crowd parts for a big, yellow dump truck. A small, smiling man with a crew cut jumps out of the cab and introduces himself—Eliasee. He laughs and pumps my father's hand. He throws our luggage into the back of the truck. We climb in after. The dump truck grinds its gears, surging up the beach and onto the one dirt road, past the two churches, the pink and blue houses that all look the same, past the Bank of Canada shaped like a huge white igloo. A packed taxi with no doors passes us. People run beside it and swing themselves on; others leap off. The taxi has no brakes, Eliasee tells us, so it doesn't stop until it runs out of gas.

Eliasee's house has a kitchen-dining-living room and two bedrooms. There is a couch, a table and not much else. It is immediately clear that Eliasee's wife and daughter do not want us here—the little girl hides from us, covering her face with her hands to make herself invisible. The woman keeps her mouth in a grim line, but Eliasee stays up every night, drinking tea, talking and laughing with my parents at the small Formica table.

Besides the priest, Eliasee is the most important man in Povungatuk. He is one of the only people in the village not on the Canadian dole. He delivers everyone's water and takes away their garbage, driving the only motor vehicle with brakes. But Mom says he is frustrated. This pond is too small for Eliasee, she says. Later, when liquor reaches Povungatuk, he will become an alcoholic, then kill himself. But now, the Canadian government still keeps alcohol out. Eliasee tells us a man has broken into the Hudson Bay Store, stolen a bottle of perfume and slugged it down, hoping to try out drunkenness.

There is not much food. A big supply ship makes its way down the bay twice a year, but it has been stuck in ice, and the ship is months late. The shelves of the Hudson Bay Store are nearly empty. There is a roast left in the store freezer, because nobody knows what to do with it. My mother cooks it for Eliasee's family. Otherwise, we mainly eat bannock, a soft white bread fried in the shape of a huge donut. We drink tea with canned sweetened, condensed milk. The toilet paper has run out too, so we wipe ourselves with catalogs. It's a little like my dad's warrior society, except there's no easy way out.

The sea washes on and on, the wind blows off the water and rustles the tundra that sweeps on and on. The tiny village huddles in between, and I am a stranger to all of it. The color of the world has narrowed. Dull green scrub, flat grey ocean, dust and pebbles and brown birds. We pick bitter white berries on the tundra, and the taste makes me lonely for Bo. The constant wind makes my eyes and nose run, as if I am always weeping. Eliasee explains that we are the first white children in the village. The Eskimo children run away from us, shrieking.

I'm having this idea that's causing me anxiety, and I try to explain it to my mother as she tucks me into Eliasee's foldout couch one night. I say, the whole world is made of little circles. She doesn't get it. I try again, There are little circles and we can't get in.

Like cells in the body? my mother asks.

But are we all one body? I wonder.

My mother tells me I'm brilliant, go to sleep.

Eliasee boats us to a rocky island to fish. I am convinced that it is the island where they keep the attack dogs, even though Eliasee says it isn't. Eliasee shows us deep fissures in the rock where people have fallen and died. I search for signs of dog. My father begins casting with his new rod and reel. Eliasee takes out a soda can with fishing line wrapped around it. Eliasee pulls in fish after fish. My father catches nothing, says nothing. My mother, my sister and I wait for the explosion. This time there isn't any, but that's almost worse.

We visit the carver's co-op. My sister is given a small piece of soapstone. We sit in front of Eliasee's house. She carves and I watch, bored and depressed. Then, two girls in red plaid shawls sidle towards us. They put their hands over their mouths and giggle at the scrapes my sister has made on her stone. Girls don't carve, they tell us.

Minnie has high cheekbones and carries her niece wrapped in a plaid shawl on her back. Mina wears bangs, is round and sweet-faced. They both have numbers instead of middle names, given to them by the Canadian government. They both wear black rubber boots over embroidered mukluks. Neither of them can stop laughing. My sister drops her stone on the doorstep, and we run off with Minnie and Mina.

Suddenly, Povungatuk is the best place on earth. We eat fried white bread and drink sweet tea all day long. The sun never sets, and we play outside past midnight under the northern lights. Mom buys us rubber boots and embroidered mukluks. When our group of girls charges through the village, I love to look down at all the identical black boots scaring up dirt. There is a movie every evening in the community center. The movies only cost a dime, and if the children don't have the change, they edge in anyway, past the blind man who collects money at the door.

Mostly, we play in a big group of girls led by Minnie and Mina, but there is a half-white girl our mother takes us to visit sometimes. Elizabee's white father worked at the Hudson Bay Store, but he is long gone. The other girls do not seem to play with Elizabee much. She looks a little like me. Elizabee and I sit quietly drinking tea in her grandmother's kitchen. She seems mournful and pale, and I prefer Minnie and Mina, who always laugh.

Eliasee takes us to meet a woman who has been in the first documentary ever made, *Nanook of the North*. Later, in college, I will finally watch the film. Nanook paddles a kayak to shore. One by one, his entire family pops out of the recesses of the boat, all huge smiles. I will feel suffocated watching the movie, imagining the whole family curled against each other inside the kayak, pressed against fur and skin.

This woman had been a little girl in the film, but now she is an old woman with no teeth. She tells winter stories of people losing their way in snowstorms, just trying to walk to their neighbor's house for a little conversation. She says that they would be found a few feet from the house, and always naked. All alone, unable to see anything but white, you go crazy. You feel hotter and hotter. You rip off all your clothes, burrow into a snowbank and fall asleep.

Finally, the supply ship breaks through the wall of ice. Everyone goes down to the shore to help unload, passing wooden crates up the beach. It is like New Year's Eve, like Thanksgiving. The whole village turns giddy, crazy for sweets. Eliasee goes to the store and comes home with four bottles of Pepsi. His wife pours pink candied popcorn into the baby's crib. The children walk around eating licorice whips and pretzel sticks. Eliasee drinks the Pepsi quickly and sends my sister and me to the store to buy more. We feel very important. On our way back with the bottles, a boy yells, Ugly white girls! He throws a stone at us.

We hug the Pepsi and run, the bottles slapping against our stomachs. Later, I tell Minnie and Mina what the boy has said, waiting for their laughter to wipe the words away. But they just shake their heads. They say that Eliasee's little girl tells everyone we are ugly white devils. I hide my pale hands in my pockets.

Then Mom asks if we would like to take an Eskimo girl home with us. Can we take Minnie and Mina both? I ask. Mom says it has to be Elizabee, because she is half-white and has a hard time of it. Her grandmother wants us to take her away for a while. I am disappointed because Elizabee is not much fun.

During the last week, Elizabee's grandmother changes her mind. She cannot part with her. The night before we leave, I go to Elizabee's to say good-bye. There is nothing in her bedroom but a couch cushion on the floor. She says, When you see a tree, kiss it for me. She smiles.

She's never seen a tree.

She tells me her favorite snack is fish eyes.

Wow. Suddenly I am in love and cannot bear to lose her. I ask if she can sleep on Eliasee's foldout couch with Beky and me on our last night in Povungatuk. She does. I realize that we are the same age, the same height, have the same long dark blond hair.

She is my twin, and when we land in Montreal, without her, the first tree I see outside the airport looks outsized, a bizarre vegetable growth. Self-consciously, I kiss it. I wonder if Elizabee can feel the rough bark on her lips.

CHAPTER FIVE

midnight hour

Winter 1971–1972

AND NOW, months later, in deep winter, we are back in our own circle, and Doug is singing for everyone. It's a talent show. He has on his dark aviator glasses, his whole body curled around an imaginary microphone. He sings in a deep gravelly voice, his face turned mysterious in shades. He feints towards us and away. He shimmies close, closer, right up into a girl's face. *I'm going to take you girl and hold you, and do all the things I told you, in the midnight hour. . . .*

I want this new Doug to sing just to me, but when he sways close, I scream and hide my face. When he edges towards my sister, she begins to sob. My father tells me to take her home to our mother. We leave the packed heat and noise and enter a night covered over in ice and frozen stars. We hold mittened hands, don't say anything, crunch over the packed snow. The woods jostle closer. An anorectic birch tree beside us moans. Maybe it's Lilith. In the old Hebrew stories, when Lilith runs away from Eden, she becomes the un-virgin who births demon girls by the thousands. The demons live in trees and lure innocents to their doom. The tree moans again. I am caught between two scary songs.

When Doug first arrived, two falls ago, we were all outside playing duck, duck, goose. A motorcycle roars over the hill, a Yamaha 650 with customized banana bars, ferrying a big guy in a leather jacket and a red, white and blue helmet. It's easy rider, someone yells. We watch as the motorcycle turns into the driveway, stops by the flags. The guy pulls off his helmet, shakes out his long dark hair. It's the new hombre! someone yells.

My father invites Doug up to the house after dinner. They sit around our long table. My mother says, Tell us about yourself. Doug looks sad but brave, just like GI Joe, and says, Some stories are hard to tell.

While they talk, my father pushes back his chair, pulls a butcher knife out of a kitchen drawer. He tests it on his thumb. Then he walks up to Doug and slashes the sleeve on his down jacket. A baggy of pills falls out.

Doug kind of chokes.

The valley is drug-free, me boy, Dad says. When my father puts his arm around him, the butcher knife still in his hand, Doug flinches. But everything is okay. My father hands out drinks, my parents asks Doug to tell his story, the real one.

I don't remember his exact words, and I can't ask him. Doug is dead. But I remember how he sounds, the rhythm of his voice, the way his fingers play nervously at the hem of his shirt. I remember his story. It goes like this:

It all started when I got busted toking up in the boy's bathroom at the Laguardia High School rock-a-thon. Not one of my brightest moves. I'm used to getting off easy, though, black Irish, million-dollar smile, everybody's favorite delinquent. So when I get to court, I start explaining right away about my miserable childhood. I concentrate on the time when I was in junior high and my mom kicked my dad out for the tenth or eleventh time. So my dad kidnapped me and flew me to France, enrolled me in a school where no one spoke English and left me there. The older Francophones screwed with me severely, since I couldn't squeal. I remained incognito for about six months, then my mom found me, and I was back in White Plains for ninth grade. French still makes me want to puke, though. I finish the story, do the smiling-through-my-tears routine and wait for the suspended sentence.

The judge takes off his glasses, he's a baldy, he wipes the crud from his eyes, gently turns his hammer over and back again. Then he starts in about a therapeutic community in the wilderness. He says there are alternatives to the system, man. I swear, he says: Man. He says I need to break the cycle of dependency on drugs. He says I need caring and love. He mentions these Monday morning meetings where students emote. He mentions building my own bed out of wood, the fruits of my own labors. It's like he's Johnny Appleseed. Then he puts his glasses on, goes legal on me. Says I have a choice, psychiatric evaluation, detox, suspension, eighty hours community service and six months probation or this hippie commune in the woods.

First thing I think of is bears and your country ax murderer types. But then I imagine myself one of these pioneer men, hunting and fishing for a living, you know, like Jeremiah Johnson.

I imagine crying in front of a bunch of people with nice faces, and I picture the weight of my slob of an old man, maybe even my habit, all rolling off my back, and I'm light, practically levitating or something.

And things weren't going so well in White Plains. No money, seems like everyone's in jail, my mom hiding her booze in the back of the toilet again and, as I remarked before, my old man won't let up. I can't go out looking the way I do after he's finished with me. Some days even my mirror shades don't do the trick. It's embarrassing.

So I say what the hell. I choose the hippies.

When I get home my dad hits me so hard he pops my zits. My mom cries. I sew a baggy of pills inside the sleeve of my coat, jump on my bike and here I am.

After Doug tells us everything, he chases me and Beky around and around the central fireplace, careful never to catch us. My parents watch and smile. We are all in love.

While it's still winter, while it snows and the wind sings through the stovepipe, I'll tell you that the way I feel about Doug with his shades on is the way I feel about animals. They are liable to do anything. I am in favor of fences, leashes, muzzles and cages. My small, frowzy-haired sister, on the other hand, is the Florence Nightingale of the animal world. She won't even let me kill a leech in a stream. She keeps cats and canaries and guinea pigs, crooning, That's okay, and chucking them under the chin. They eventually die, and then she sadly buries them out back.

Once, she's cradling her cat when a dog rushes them. The cat claws its way up my sister's shoulder, while my sister keeps the dog at bay. The deep scratch heals badly, leaving her at the age of six with a puffy four-inch keloid scar on her upper arm, the mark of her ferocious devotion.

One day, I tell my father that while I was bending over her feed bucket, my goat, Fern, knocked me down and put her hard little hooves on my back, pressing against me. My father thinks this is hilarious, makes jokes about randy as a goat, says Fern is trying to mount me. I thought Fern was a girl. I no longer want anything to do with him. Eventually, Fern disappears.

Just getting in and out of the log cabin is like an episode from *Wild Kingdom.* Swallows build their nests inside the mud-room. I cower, cover my head with my hands and make a rush for the front door. The swallows dive-bomb me as I cross the threshold.

For a while, mysteriously, every time I leave the house I get stung by a wasp. My mother rubs butter on the sting. That doesn't help much. I always use my father's five-leaf cure instead. By the time I find the five varieties of vegetation and squish them in my palm, the sting is gone. Finally, we discover that the wasps have built their nests in the bells that hang on the front door.

Every time I open the door, the bells jingle, and the wasps attack. Still, this doesn't explain why it is just me who is stung.

And the Scotch Highland cattle, they're pretty to look at, with their burnt orange hair. But their horns are curved and pointed as spears, and I am afraid to get too near them. One time, Giovanni gets steamed, charges out to the field and punches a cow. He breaks his hand on the cow's forehead. I don't even like to cross the field where the cattle are penned. It creeps me out, the way they all swing their heads up and watch with their big cow eyes.

Doug asks me if I want to help bring hay to the cows on the tractor. I agree, because I love both Doug and the tractor. We trundle out to the field, then lower the hay from the front bucket onto the ground. The cows sidle up from all corners of the field, surrounding us. They lash their tails, toss their horns, bellow and chew. While Doug laughs, I climb onto his shoulders, terrified.

We have another Newfoundland for a while, Panda's son, a huge grey dog named Sam Maguilicutty, but Sam is much worse than no dog at all. Sam looks just as droopy as Panda, but his hobby is killing barnyard fowl. For a while, Sam divides his time between offing ducks and chickens and moping around with a dead chicken tied around his neck. My father thinks this is a good cure for his fowl habit. Sam looks as limp as the dead chicken, but he still likes live ones. After a while, Sam disappears.

My father, I assume, prefers to kill the chickens himself. We watch him slaughter them with an ax. He tells us the chickens will chase us after they are killed, in revenge for their untimely deaths. We scoff. You can't put that one over on us. He demonstrates. He chops the head off a chicken, then hurls the struggling body towards us. The headless whirling ball of maroon feathers and blood tumbles over itself, trying to get us. We scream and run, but we edge back to watch the rest of the slaughter.

Winter. I'm watching Angie press on Doug's crotch. We're in the main house, they're sitting together on a sunken couch. He's wailing that he has to pee, squeezing his knees together. She keeps pressing down there with the palm of her hand. I laugh, too, but I can't figure out why Doug doesn't just get up and go to the bathroom.

When we're alone, Angie tells me the story of her romance with Doug. One of the teachers arranges a meeting with Angie and the boys she has slept with. It takes place in Angie's bedroom on the second floor of the main house. There are boys leaning nervously on the bed and boys twitching their legs in folding chairs. They are supposed to talk about why she sleeps with men who don't love her. But Doug speaks up from his folding chair: I love you, Angie. Meeting over. I remember her smile when she tells this part, like Sleeping Beauty, sweet, groggy and unsurprised.

I picture this love story over and over, especially the part when Doug says, I love you, Angie.

We drive to Glens Falls each Friday night to assuage our cabin fever. We are allowed to choose either a movie or roller-skating. I always choose roller-skating. I roll around the edges under the whirling rainbow lights, watching the couples skate-dance to Three Dog Night's "Joy to the World" or John Denver's "Country Roads." I know all the words to both songs.

On the long drive home, Doug holds me in his lap while I pretend to sleep. My mother is in the front passenger seat, I can see her through my slit eyes. The van's windows are steamed over with our collective breath. Doug's arms are gentle, his chest is warm, his lap is hard down there. I want this van ride to last forever.

We're in the drafty main house at night. I'm cold. The men and boys have all gone off somewhere with my father, and the women are hanging out in front of the woodstove. One of the boyfriends Bo's mother, Ellen, has met through the personals is here. He's a trucker, and his rig is parked by the trailer. Now, he and Ellen are standing in the corner, arguing in tense, hushed voices. We all pretend not to notice.

He starts hitting her. It is quick and inevitable, like a one-sided boxing match. He grunts with the effort, his fists hammering her shoulders, face and belly. Someone screams. Everyone jumps back, including the other teachers. Mom pulls Beky and me behind the table and grips our shoulders.

Kitty jams herself between Ellen and the man beating her. Kitty's forearms are in front of herself like a shield, her deep, calm voice repeats, Leave her alone, now. He backs off, curses the general room, Cunts. He slams the front door as he leaves. In a few minutes we hear the growl as his eighteen-wheeler pulls out. The room fills back up with air. Kitty is fifteen years old.

Finally, it's mud season again. On the first day of sun and snowmelt, my father sets speakers up outside the house, then fills the valley with sweet waves of Vaughn Williams's "Lark Ascending." We all toss off our coats and run outside, shivering in our T-shirts. Despite the romantic music, there is no real spring in the Adirondacks, no flowering magnolias or forsythia, no pastel season at all. Fragile grass pushes up under brittle, tawny straw. Deer eat the few scrawny tulips and daffodils. Wet wind. Everything the bright snow has hidden, revealed—dog shit, lost combs, moldering hats and gloves and milk cartons. Blackflies cake our faces. Mud season is the high and the low. A membrane of blue sky trembling above, below, a roiling mess as the earth wrestles winter off.

One evening in late spring, we are in our fort, underneath the dome porch. We make up a secret language in which you mumble everything on an exhale of breath. We see a light in the main dining room. Let's-see-who-that-is. We crowd around a window. Inside, Ann is lying on a table. Doug is on top of her. We jostle to get a look, pour out excitement in our secret gasping language. They notice our faces at the window, laugh, then put on a show for us. We stand on tiptoe in the dark, watching them have sex on the table.

I can't figure this Doug and Ann thing out. Doug's real girlfriend, Angie, is like a princess, like a Barbie, she is serene, she has a little upturned nose, she even rides a white horse. Ann is all skin and bones and buckteeth. Ann spits and scratches. Why would Doug want to have sex with Ann?

If, at that moment, I had turned away from the lighted window, looked into the background, into Bo's shadowed face, what would I have seen? Could I have read my best friend's eyes and understood what he couldn't tell me? That Doug and Ann force him up to the hayloft, make him suck them and touch them. They hurt him, then they threaten him never to tell or else. That right now, this spring, they are changing him forever.

But I didn't look at him, and I didn't know, wouldn't know until I was twenty years too late to help.

Now, unknowing, I wonder if Doug and I will have sex on our date when I am eighteen.

About a week later, I am sitting beside Doug in a truck. He says he has to go on an errand in town for my father, and I jokingly refuse to leave the cab. He looks at me then, his eyes focused suddenly, instead of glinting off like they usually do. Come with me, he says. That look is too strong.

No. I scramble out of the truck and run for my mother.

We sleep over at Bo's house, wake in the morning to find Ellen in bed with Brad. We come home and my father is cuddling with Laurie on the bed. My sister goes downstairs one night and finds Paul and my mother entangled on the floor.

What does it feel like to live in a world without monogamy? Do my mother and Laurie sit together and whisper secrets about the men they share, wicked giggling that makes my father and Paul wince and check their machinery?

Or, say it's mud season, a day when there's a cool, wet wind, and the crocuses are pushing through, my mother and Paul run off into the woods, do what they want and now emerge through some birch trees, holding hands, a few new leaves pasted in their hair, the seats and cuffs of their jeans muddy. Here's my father. Do Paul and my mother flinch, drop hands? Does my father laugh angrily? Or, does he simply take my mother's hand, or even Paul's, and the three of them walk together in the weak spring sunshine, like Adam and Eve and Lilith in an Eden God never imagined.

That's about as far as my imagination will take me into these affairs. If this were fiction, I'd have to distance my mother and Paul to write a sex scene. Make them both blond and tall, from Iowa. But, as a child, I don't pay attention to the specific gestures of their romance, anyway. Watching my mother and father kiss, or my mother and Paul, makes me wince, look away, but I know, that's what grown-ups do.

I am more interested in my own sex games. When Bo sleeps over, we lie together in my single bed. We are in our underwear, discussing various things, like new fort ideas, how one might build a Barbie torture chamber, the ingredients of hobo stew. Then Bo asks me if I want to fuck.

No, I say. I understand the rudiments of sexual intercourse, and I have a vague sense that the penis thing would hurt.

Come on, he says, I've fucked before. With a girl that lives near my father.

Liar. The idea that he knows someone from outside the valley is preposterous.

I did. Her name is River.

I am jealous, but not inclined to repeat River's mistake. I feign a huge yawn. I'm going to sleep.

A few weeks later, I relent. We are all on a double mattress on the edge of the sleeping loft over the living room—Beky, Bo and I. We decide to take turns. I let Beky go first, see how she fares. Bo lies inertly on top of her in his underpants.

That's it? I thought Bo understood the secret of real sex, but now I realize he only wants to have sex the Barbie, GI Joe way. I wonder smugly if he even knows how the real thing goes. I have no idea how heroic he is, lying gently on top and not passing on the brutality he's been taught.

Each one of us gets a turn, then we begin to discuss who is the best at fucking. Suddenly, there is a great burst of laughter from downstairs. We stare at each other. The adults have heard everything. We dive under the covers, as if the blankets can shield us from humiliation.

The valley teenagers, with their long greasy hair, their dirty T-shirts, gold chains and mudcaked bell-bottoms, their cigarettes and knowing laughter, seem to understand sex inside out and backwards. They know sex so well, it almost bores them. I expect when I become a teenager, and start dating Doug or Michael Jackson, sex will become second nature for me, too.

But for now, I hope to be as smooth and hard as a plastic doll, and just as unreachable. I like the ordered idea of sex as two unmoving objects pressed together.

Dad says we're going to have a pig roast to celebrate the warm weather. My sister and I follow him down to the pigpen. While he's gathering students and tools together, we play with the pigs. We climb up their fence, then jump down and sprint through the muck for the other side. The pigs gallop after us. I don't know what they would have done if they caught us. We always won.

My father is ready now. He shoots the pig in the head outside the pen. The other pigs trot around behind the fence, squealing nervously. The pig jerks, her legs running as she lies on her side. I wonder if people run like that when they die. Then my father sticks a hook in her back and winches her up, lowers her into the vat of boiling water, winches her out and slits her open from neck to anus. He pulls back the two flaps as if he were opening a door. I watch all this from a distance of a few feet, fascinated. Surrounded by teenaged boys and other teachers, my father cuts with his butcher's knife, pulling out bean-colored organs and intestines that hang from his hands in heavy coils. He takes his knife to the pig's head. Then, he turns to me.

The pig's tongue, nine inches long, hangs from his clenched teeth. He comes towards me, snorting. I run. He chases me across the field. I am screaming my head off, imagining the warm, thick feel of that tongue on my neck. I can see my mother seated on the steps of the dome, and I lunge for her. I throw myself on her. She admonishes my father mildly. He takes the tongue out, laughs, gets back to work.

That night, for the pig roast, Dad dresses Mom up in a sheet that drapes from one shoulder to her waist, exposing a breast. He paints the bare breast with paisley reds and blues. At that pig roast my mom begins to smell of rum. I watch my perpetually composed mother sway with her own giddiness, her eyes strange and shiny, the paint on her breast smeared with a handprint. Paul is always near my mother. I don't know where my father and Laurie are.

To get my mother's attention, I cup her chin and pull her face towards me, but her eyes list away. I try another standard trick, call my mother's name in a sharp, grown-up voice. I try to call her back to herself and to me, but on this day, she will not come.

I climb the stairs to my room. I take out the collection of hand-me-down Playboy centerfolds my father has given me. I study these nude centerfolds with reliably identical bodies, all tanned, smooth and unblemished as my Barbies. Here, the world is still in order. This comforts me.

But what about you? Are you tired of my urge for order? Are you tired of women and children and winter and mud season all together? Are you ready for a man's adventure? A Royal Navy trip is about to depart. My father, Doug and Paul leave first in a pickup truck. They're carrying twenty dozen eggs. You and the others follow a half hour later in the van, with your own cache of eggs. The van turns a corner, and there's the empty truck blocking the road.

Grab a carton of eggs, yank open the van door, duck your head. Bellow, Attack! and run out into the ambush. It's an all-out egg battle for an hour. Laugh so hard it hurts.

After the eggs, this Royal Navy trip goes on as usual for a while, you're swigging rum, setting off cannons in the middle of the ocean, almost drowning every day and then, somehow, at the end of a bleary, drunken week, you end up in Montreal.

You all check into some sleazy dive. Come home late from carousing—Paul, the admiral, Doug and you. You're stumbling down a narrow hallway to your rooms, dressed in your white sailor pants, navy wool coats with gold buttons, swords, the admiral in his whole getup, stockings, etc.,...when down the hall come some genuine Canadian sailors, in genuine uniforms.

They block the way.

What the fuck are you supposed to be? one of them says, and they all snicker.

The admiral replies, Her Majesty's royal naval officers. Stand aside.

A sailor says, Are you pussies fucking with the navy?

The admiral says, Draw your swords, gentlemen.

You all look at him.

Draw your swords, he slurs again in his English accent.

You draw your swords. The swords make that shriek they do when they come out of the scabbard. Are you holding the sword correctly? Look at Doug. That big dumb grin on his face.

Stand aside, the admiral repeats.

There's this moment of nothing, the swords out, quivering a little, impatient. You can't even see the enemies' faces in the dark hallway. This hall is so close and hot, it's hard to breathe.

Then the sailors shrug, say something like, Wackos, loonies, just get out of our fucking way.

They're gone, you can put your sword away.

Maybe this is getting a little too real.

CHAPTER SIX

the last battle

1973

WE HAVE a small black-and-white television that sits on a dresser above my parents' bed, the only television in the valley. By twisting a wire hanger, we can sometimes get channel three. While my father lies in bed with a slipped disc, we run home after school and watch *Wild, Wild West* and *Bonanza* with him. We sit there at the end of the bed, kicking our heels against the mattress, our backs companionably to my father. We accept the fact that he is always in bed when we get home. I imagine this is his afternoon nap, and I assume it is a British custom. (I assume everything that is inscrutable about my father is due to his Englishness. Those wacky British people.) I don't realize he has taken to bed full-time since that pig roast, four months now. He says his back hurts. Although she doesn't tell me then, my mother thinks he is restless and depressed about Paul and my mother's affair.

Today, Toby, Les's son, says he wants to watch, too. Toby is a good-looking, curly haired boy. Small for his age, he walks on his toes. He often refuses to be part of the program, which irritates Bo and me, the king and queen of the Little School. He follows us up the hill to the log cabin.

I don't know, I say, there might not be enough room on the bed.

He stands in front of me. You can't stop me. It's not your television.

I shove my hands on my hips. What are you talking about? We own everything. My father could kick you off this land anytime he wants to.

My father says pretty soon we're all going to own the land together. It's only fair.

Oh, really? Well, if you want to watch *Bonanza,* you're going to have to pay me a dime.

Beky and Bo snicker.

Toby hesitates.

I put my hand out in front of him. Pay up, I say.

He fishes in his tight, high-water jeans and brings out the dime. I drop the dime in my jewelry box when we get inside, and we all head over to the bed.

I especially love the beginnings of *Wild, Wild West* and *Bonanza*, the sudden flare-ups of violence. At the beginning of *Wild, Wild West*, a cartoon cowboy kisses a lady, quickly punches her, then leans jauntily against the wall for a smoke. On *Bonanza*, the guys ride in on horseback, galloping to the rousing music. Suddenly, the picture begins to flame at the edges, until the whole screen burns to a crisp.

A few months later, in late winter, my father gets out of bed and goes to Montreal where an Asian man sticks needles in his back. He seems to be cured. Now, my father can watch his beloved cowboys on the big screen. He takes me to the Schroon Lake theater to see John Wayne movies. We are often the only ones in the audience. The movie theater has no heat, so they hand out blankets. They sell used furniture as a sideline. Old chairs and tables and bureaus crowd the aisles of the theater, so you have to climb over them to get into your seat. The John Wayne movies are full of bullets, blood flowering on chests, cowboys groaning and keeling over; but the more killing, the more my father laughs and squeezes my hand, to let me know it is all an absurd and wonderful game.

We're driving to Glens Falls in the yellow van. The bus is crowded with rowdy students. This will probably be our last trip for the year because it is spring, snow melting, and these trips are meant to fend off cabin fever. We bump down the dirt road, the staff driver, Brad, pushing the gas hard. The teenagers love speed, egg him on. They whoop as we sail off the hills, our stomachs lifting.

When we near the waterfalls, I see a woman with long red hair sitting on a chair in the middle of the first bridge, painting on an easel. As the van rushes towards her, she turns, her paintbrush poised. Brad wrenches the wheel to the right. We skid past the painter, miss the second bridge and slide down the embankment towards the swollen stream.

The van stops, tilted on the bank, wheels in mud, the right windows just above the water. For a minute there is breath-holding silence. Then giddy laughter. The sliding door won't open because it's on the stream side. The teenagers start rocking the van, laughing, catcalling, trying to get it to tip. Brad yells at them.

I panic. The passenger windows won't open wide enough to crawl through, so I scramble over Brad and leap out the driver's side window.

My sister remembers that it is Kitty who pushes us through the van window. I have no memory of this. My whole self was focused towards escape, but I can picture her smooth, strong arms catapulting us to safety.

Afterwards, I dream of bridges collapsing, of our car plunging into deep water, of driving off a cliff into empty air. At night, I close my eyes and have visions under my lids. The dark resolves itself into a black stick figure dropping at a great rate through black clouds, clouds too insubstantial to halt the careening. I begin to dislike the story of Icarus.

Les and my father can't agree about ownership of the school. Les wants everyone to buy into the property, so we can achieve common ownership. He's built a house, the bunker, but my parents own it. People are taking sides. Paul and Laurie are clearly with my parents. Brad is in the middle. He wants joint ownership, but he and my father have the same sense of humor. They go around cackling, doing their villain routine. There are staff meetings. Les makes impassioned arguments for joint ownership, the creation of a truly egalitarian community. My father yells and storms out. My mother smooths things over. Les throws up his hands. I can't fight this, Les says to everyone. They're like a two-headed monster.

I can't ride my horse Pepper anymore, she's too wild since Ann got hold of her. I watch Ann tear across the fields on Pepper, Ann's feet jostling close to the ground, her hoop earrings spinning wildly as she whips the reins. I hear Mom murmur something about the fact that Ann is ruining Pepper.

Stop her, I say, it's my horse. But no one stops her, everyone has to express themselves in the valley, and Pepper's expressions grow wilder. Toby has a little red horse cart and decides to hitch Pepper to it. Pepper bolts. We watch the black-and-white pony drag Toby and his little red cart furiously over the hill. They disappear. Pepper takes off a few more times with us kids. Pepper disappears for good.

That spring break, the whole staff goes to a conference in the city. They leave my father to baby-sit eight children. He loads us all into the station wagon and takes us to the drive-in to see *Planet of the Apes*. I don't like that planet. Those talking apes scare me, and Charlton Heston is always grimacing and escaping, with scary music in the background. I climb into the back of the wagon to get away from the movie. Curled on the floor, draped over the backseat, sprawled in the back, we all eventually fall asleep to the staticky sound of the apes and the humans battling for control of the planet.

We are in the Little School, it's raining and Ellen has been reading to us for hours. We have come to the last book in C. S. Lewis's Narnia series. The ending of this book, *The Last Battle*, ruins me. The good guys lose the battle, then suddenly find themselves in a paradise, where they reunite with the characters from all the books. But then they realize they're dead. They're not upset. C. S. Lewis writes that "it's the beginning of the greatest adventure of all," but not for me. Ellen reads the last words, closes the book and we are shut out.

We stare at her, dazed and disappointed. Look, she says, It stopped raining. Why don't you go out and play?

We stumble into the field in front of the Little School, blinking our eyes in the sun. Bo and I decide to play cowboys and Indians. We divide up the rest of the kids, Indians here, cowboys over there.

I'll be a monkey, Toby says, standing on his toes.

There's no monkeys in cowboys and Indians, Bo says.

You can call me Monkey Roo, Toby says.

Choose a cowboy or an Indian, my voice rises, or you can't play.

It's a free country, Toby says.

Fine! I yell, Fucking Monkey Roo. Guess what? We're going to call you Monkey Fuck!

Get him, Bo yells.

Toby assesses the situation and takes off across the field. All of us are chasing him, kids from three years old to eight. He's heading for the trees, near Bo's trailer. He reaches a slim poplar and shimmies up the trunk above our heads.

We chant, Monkey Fuck, Monkey Fuck. We all push against the tree, trying to shake him out.

Bo runs into the trailer and comes out with an ax. He chops at the tree to the rhythm of our chanting, Monkey Fuck, Monkey Fuck.

But cutting down a tree is slow going, and our chant eventually fades away. Bo stops hacking and drops the ax, breathing hard. It's a muggy day, we realize, there are blackflies in halos around our heads. Plus, we've already missed *Wild, Wild West,* and our jeans are sodden to the knees from running through wet grass. If we hurry, we'll catch *Bonanza.*

Toby must have climbed down the tree sometime after.

My father and Brad plan a war, Romans and Celts. My father must have felt like taking it easy, because he opts to base the Celts at the main house while the Romans must invade from the woods. As usual, Doug, Giovanni and Paul end up on his side. The Romans, led by Brad and Les, consist of schizophrenics, paranoids and sensitive bookworms. My mother has always acted as the Red Cross or its equivalent, but this time she opts out of the whole enterprise. Maybe she's finally growing tired of smoothing things over.

The Romans leave for the woods, dressed in their Roman uniforms from the theatrical supply company in New York City. It is agreed that the battle will start the next morning. While the Romans make camp, the Celts build a pagan shrine out of two-by-fours on the hill. Like everything my father builds, it goes up quickly and has style; a blond airy shell through which you can see the sky. Then they roast a pig, which takes all night. They eat it at sunrise.

Toby has gone with his father to be a Roman, but Bo, my sister and I are just spectators, so we watch the first confrontation from the lawn. The Romans march out of the woods in formation.

The Celts wait in front of the barn, dressed in feed sacks held together with baling twine. Their capes are old blankets. They smell of wood smoke and Cutter's insect repellent. Between every second Celt is a feed pail filled with plastic bags of cow shit. Each bag has a yard of baling twine attached to it. There are also three dead rats knotted to more twine. Everyone has leering grins on their faces. Giovanni has filled a football full of gunpowder, with a short fuse sticking out.

Bo and Beky and I are hopping up and down, jostling each other, mumbling, Come on, come on.

The Romans strike up their drums, cross the field in formation, and move onto the dirt road. My father has set a stake about thirty yards from the barn. The Romans give a cheer and start to charge, lobbing firecrackers as they run.

As the Romans reach the stake, my father yells, Fire!, and each Celt twirls a bag full of cow shit around his head and lets go. Bags of shit and the three rats sail through the air. A yell of dismay rises from the Roman army. But the Romans keep coming. Firecrackers are popping, people screaming, balloons bursting, shit and water running down faces.

Someone throws a lit firecracker into the satchel of gunpowder Doug carries on his back. It explodes, he yells, pulls off the backpack, burning his arm. Shit, he groans, shit, shit.

Then suddenly, unbelievably, it looks like the Romans have the Celts on the run. They chase the Celts up the dirt road, through the fields, past the pagan shrine. We chase after them. Up Ceremony Hill, which is the boundary they have set for the game. The Romans have them cornered now. But the Celts, led by my father, crash through a stand of pine trees and down the slope behind. Les yells angrily, Out of bounds!

But Brad and the others are already following the Celts down the incline. We skid after them, whooping. As soon as we're in the gully we realize it is an ambush. Celts appear from all along the ridge above. Firecrackers and shit begin to rain down on us.

I watch Giovanni edging towards us. He grins, lights a match on the zipper of his jeans and starts the firecrackers he holds in his hand.

You can't get us, I yell, We're not part of the game.

He throws the firecrackers at us anyway. My sister starts to scream. A firecracker has gone down her shirt and is burning her. Bo shakes it out onto the ground.

Dad! I yell, Dad!

He comes over, glances at us, pats Beky's head. Take your sister home, he says.

Wait, Dad, Giovanni—I begin, but my father is already gone. Bo and I bring her up to the log cabin. While she examines Beky's burn, my mother glances accusingly out the window, as if she can see my father running through the woods, breaking rules.

After Beky stops crying, we walk down the hill from the log cabin. The pagan shrine is in flames. The Romans have burned it on their retreat. I feel sad, watching it turn to ash. The Celts have gathered down at the main house again. My father laughs angrily as we watch the last of the Romans shrieking and tearing back into the woods, waving their torches.

That night, my father stirs a big pot on the stove at the main house. As he stirs, he does his villain cackle, the one he and Brad like to do. He makes pemmican, a variation on a kind of Native American beef jerky, to which he adds raisins and chocolate to the meat and lard. He sends the pemmican out to the Romans as a goodwill gesture. Then, that same night, my father moves his operations out of the main house and into the woods at the far end of the valley.

The pemmican is made with Ex-lax. All the Romans get violently ill. Toby is out there. Eight years old, he spends the night leaning against a tree, crouched over with cramps and diarrhea.

Early next morning, Bo, Beky and I come down the hill from the log cabin. Brad and Les are messing with the flags. They have pulled down the English flag and strung up some shit-covered underwear. Then, they run over to my father's bell tower and pour gasoline all over the base. They light it. The fire growls up the tower. Brad is doing the cackle, but it sounds more like a screech. We watch in silence. They are still shrieking laughter as they grab their gas can and run for the woods.

We are the holders of vital information. We race down the logging road to my father's camp. We are a little afraid to go this way, because we know there are crazy teenagers all over the woods, and because we have to pass the dump, a notorious hangout for black bears. But the teenagers must have frightened off the bears. At the end of the logging road we are stopped by a wall of barbed wire. Giovanni yells at us, Spies! Get out of here!

We're not spies! We have to see my dad. Giovanni holds up some of the wire and we crawl through. We walk by Doug, who is dressing his burnt arm. My father comes over. He looks impatient. We tell him, our voices breathy with excitement. He doesn't laugh. His face clenches.

The Roman-Celt battle abruptly ends, but the valley war keeps going. The week after, clots of tense grown-ups sit in circles that suddenly erupt in yelling. At one meeting, my father shouts at Brad, while Brad cries. Finally, they work out some sort of cease-fire.

It's May, Angie is riding her horse across the newly green fields. She is so beautiful on her galloping white horse. Her long, wheat-colored hair streams out behind her. Then the horse stumbles, Angie flies over its head. She lands on her own head in the grass. She moans.

Brad and Doug come up the hill to the log cabin. My father is there, cleaning his gun with shammy cloth. Brad and Doug say that Angie has hit her head riding, she has thrown up, they need to take her to the hospital. My father asks a few questions about the accident. He says, I've had a lot of experience with head trauma during the war. She doesn't need to go to the hospital.

Doug says, Come on, man, we're just going to have her checked out.

My father looks up from the gun, No.

We're taking her, Brad says.

If you take her you're fired.

With a strangled bellow, Brad leaps on my father's back. The gun skids into the corner. My father is twisting and bucking, they're both grunting, Brad has his hands around my father's neck. Finally Brad falls off, stumbles against the log wall.

We're taking her to the hospital, Brad gasps.

You're fired, my father says. He looks at Doug.

Doug looks at the ground. We're just going to have her checked out, Doug mumbles. He follows Brad out the door.

That night we are eating dinner, just the four of us, in the log cabin. The black rotary by the table keeps ringing. First it's Doug. Angie has a mild concussion. She just needs bedrest. My mother speaks soothingly. Then there are more calls, from Brad and Les. I can hear their tiny, outraged voices. My mother tries to soothe them, too. We're just settling back to our plates when the phone rings again. Before my mother can answer, my dad jumps up. His chair skids across the floor. He rips the phone out of the wall, takes it to the door and heaves it into the driveway. Then he grabs his rifle. He shoots it, again and again.

My mother begins to cry. My sister and I look at each other and laugh from where we are crouching under the table, our hearts chuckling in our chests.

Next day, we're hanging out on the front cinder-block steps of Bo's trailer.

Toby walks up. We're leaving, he says.

Where are you going?

We're moving away. So is Brad, pretty much everyone is leaving.

We can't think what to say.

Good, Bo finally says.

Yeah, good, I echo.

With a few weeks to go in the school year, the remaining staff members decide to take students on trips. My parents bring a group of students to camp on a small island off the coast of Maine. On the island is a cannery, fishermen, gorse bushes and wild beaches.

It rains for a week straight. We are mildewed, cold and dispirited. My father sees a poster in town for a free dinner at the local high school, sponsored by the Republican party.

In the fall, we will have a popular vote in the valley, and McGovern will win. I will vote for McGovern and will be pleased by his victory, but not surprised. I will feel a little sorry for Nixon. He has a big nose, and he doesn't even receive one vote.

Back on the island, we arrive at the public high school for our free dinner. We walk down the empty, dimly lit halls. All of us, wild-haired, in wet jeans, smelling of sweat, mold and smoke, crowd around the door of the cafeteria to take a look. Obviously, we are late.

I feel like the little match girl, gazing in at the warmth, the light and the glitter. Long tables covered with starched white cloth, glowing in the fluorescent light. Men in dark suits. And the women! I'd thought only Barbies got to wear dresses like that.

Flashing sequined gowns, stiletto-heeled pumps. Hair ballooning over their heads in stiff wiglike splendor. A man with a crew cut is already at the podium, holding forth into a microphone.

I press back against the pressure of students pushing me into the cafeteria. Free or not, it is clear we are uninvited. I hear a low-voiced discussion about whether we should go in, probably my mother saying, No, my father saying, Yes. We go in. They are already clearing the tables, but they bring us white china plates. We scrape our metal folding chairs in and out. I don't think there is much food left. I don't remember the lasagna or spaghetti pie, the soft white bread and melting margarine or the chicken divan or pineapple-topped ham. I remember the heat in the room, from food, from people and from tension. We leave in the middle of a speech. As we walk down the hall, the students jittery and loud-mouthed in the echoey silence, I see a red lever on the wall. I stop to investigate. I have just learned to read, and happily, I sound out, PULL. So, I do.

A huge pulsing honk fills the halls. I realize I've done something seriously wrong. A lot of the teenagers tear out of the building. I trust their instincts for flight. I run with them. The sequined women and suited men begin to stream out of the cafeteria. We hear the fire engine sirens approaching.

One of the students tells on me. My mother stands in the drizzle, lit up by red flashing lights, and explains what has happened to a Republican official, and then to a fireman. The Republicans return to their convention. I don't go to jail. My mother gently explains fire alarms.

We go back to our drenched tents on the beach, shaking our heads at these island people who are so out of touch with the times.

CHAPTER SEVEN

the marriage of boadicea and abraham lincoln

1953–1963

WHEN MY MOTHER was an adolescent in Brooklyn, she was no beauty. To hide her acne, she wore a thick beige foundation on her round face. To hide the hair on her upper lip, she bleached it with peroxide, leaving her skin red and peeling under a thick white mustache. This was the early fifties, so she home-permed her hair, wore blouses with starched Peter Pan collars and thick brown skirts below the knee. She dated ugly, earnest Jewish boys that she met at socialist summer camp.

On dates, she and her boyfriends would watch flickering black-and-white newsreels of bulldozers shoveling mountains of dirt and dead Jews, the twisted limbs white, the world black around them. Her father told her about his murdered grandfather and cousins, about his Chasidic childhood, the laundry slung across courtyards, the yeshivas and the gossip. The people were all gone, the laundry piled in unsorted mounds; only a few stories were recovered, brittle pages buried in tin boxes.

But there was still hope. My mother watched Technicolor footage of the communal farms in the new state of Israel, people as young as herself in shorts and blue beanies, smiling and picking bright oranges from green trees. She could imagine the firm feel of the new fruit in her hand.

First Chasidim, then socialists, then beatniks, then hippies, now feminists, lesbians, reconstructionist Jews—my mother's family has always been swept away with the newest possibility of making the world a little sweeter. In Hebrew it's called *Tikkun olam*: The world is broken, and it's our job to repair it. *Tikkun olam* is the secret to our Jewish nature, mournful because we live in a shattered world, buoyant because we believe it's possible to glue the pieces back together. But whether we are rocked in the ark of history or the times grow rough, and we founder, we are always the chosen, the first ones He asks to dance. We wear His corsage on our wrists.

Equally important in understanding how my mother continued to believe in the rightness of her vision, even as things went wrong, is this: as a teenager, she had a print of Abraham Lincoln in a socialist realist style over her bed. He was her ideal human: a martyr with mournful eyes, a working man with callused hands, tall, never told a lie, a book lover who read in his log cabin by candlelight far into the night. He raised up the downtrodden, even though he had to become a dictator to do it. He married a crazy woman. He maintained order while the country imploded. He refused to allow separation.

My mother took after Honest Abe. Like Abe, she was nothing if not good, cared for the downtrodden and her younger sisters while her Polish father spent his days as a cutter in the garment district and his nights as a union organizer, while her beautiful Russian mother moaned, I can't take it anymore, and collapsed on the couch. She lived at home and went to Brooklyn College at age sixteen, studying special education. Each Saturday night she squeezed on her girdle, snapped on her garters, had nervous diarrhea; then she and her date took the subway to Manhattan. Back in Brooklyn, she necked on the couch after dates until her father called from upstairs, It's getting late.

My mother turned eighteen. Her skin cleared up, electrolysis zapped off her mustache, she grew her hair into that long, dark braid. It became clear that she had a tiny waist, fragile wrists and ankles, a huge smile. She turned beatnik, wearing black skirts and sweaters and olive berets and snapping her fingers at poetry readings in the Village. She still watched movies about kibbutzim in Israel and dreamed of starting her own communal school. That summer of her eighteenth year, she went to work at a camp in the Catskills for disturbed children.

On my father's side, I come from a long line of liars. My father's family has always relied on fiction and charisma to overcome poverty, homeliness, the law and the facts. My father says we were British witches, second sight passed on through the female line, my father the male exception that proves the rule. These witches can invent the future before it happens. But don't imagine Glinda the Good Witch, though we resemble her in the face, or the Wicked Witch of the West either, though conflagration is a family tradition. A real witch is not interested in good or evil. Real witchery is only about desire.

Let me illustrate. According to my father, his grandmother was a midwife, his grandfather a postman. This was somewhere in the British Isles, somewhere in the first decade of the twentieth-century. The Tubb family lived in a gamekeeper's cottage on the edge of a great estate.

Let's call it Primavera Cottage, recalling aristocratic travels in Spain. Because of its name, it is always spring there: wet and neon green, calyxes bursting, low-slung budding branches, hermaphroditic slugs impregnating each other in the moss. Rotting red roses crawl over the moldy stone cottage all the way up to the thatched roof. Pollen drifts.

From photographs, I know Mister Tubb, my great-grandfather, has a dark, walrus mustache, big ears, squinty eyes, a narrow, elegant nose. I imagine he wears postal blue, has a cap and rides a bicycle. Home from work, he props his black bicycle against the stone wall, carries meat pasties, the white parcel tied with string, one side of the stiff paper wet through with warm grease. He ducks to enter the cottage. Inside, his daughter Doris has already lit the oil lamps and set the table with chipped crockery. My grandmother has a delicate face and a long, rangy body, her father's fine nose. She looks a little like an Afghan hound.

After dinner, Doris will heat the kettle for tea, and her

mother, Mrs. Tubb, will arrive. She is an ample woman pressed into a tight, burgundy silk dress. Her dark hair in a knot at the top. She wears a brooch, has a sweet, double-chinned face. She always brings delicacies—quince jelly, cognac, Devonshire cream. The whole family is greedy for treats.

She is often rushed though, on these evening visits. Mrs. Tubb sitting on the edge of the dining room chair gulping the last of her tea, talking business: Doris's dress needs to be let out, the roses have blight, may I see the grocery bill. But Mister Tubb is a mild man who likes his tea, so he doesn't argue, just sips on, nodding slowly. He is slightly vain about his mustache but otherwise humble. He deeply loves comfort, and he is deeply in love with his childhood sweetheart, his wife, Mrs. Tubb. He takes what he can get.

So when Mrs. Tubb kisses him quickly, wipes a little cream off his mustache, he nods again, lets her go. But Doris, my grandmother, is another story. She watches from the window, clenching her buckteeth, watches the generous shape of her mother disappear up the drive, back to the mansion. Doris is one long sear of jealousy.

Doris runs out of the house, her father calls, Close the door, there's a good girl. She doesn't close the door. Mister Tubb gets up to latch it himself, mutters, Doris is an odd duck.

Doris runs, shedding pinafore, dress, drawers. She is a naked thirteen-year-old girl in an ancient forest of oak trees, and she is breathing hard. She throws herself down in front of her favorite tree. She likes this one because the roots look like arms in a ropy embrace. She slides into the circle of roots. She uses her magic trick to rid herself of bad thoughts. She doesn't look, but she touches herself down there. She gets wilder and wilder with jeal-

ousy, and then magic, all gone. It is just now, my father says, as
Doris lies panting peacefully, that the tree gods and goddesses
reveal themselves to her for the first time.

Meanwhile, you can guess what happens when Mrs. Tubb
reaches the mansion, can't you? She tells the butler he can lock
up, climbs the great staircase to her room. The heavy hair comes
down, it has a natural wave. The wine-colored dress pulls up
over her head, the corset cracks open—out pop her large pale
breasts bitten red by the stays. Naked, she lies back on the bed.
The lord of the manor enters in his silk robe. He hangs it behind
the door. She smiles, he smiles, his ruddy body pushes inside her
pale one. We have desire, we have disorder, we have the cottage
thrown in rent-free, and they are both very well pleased.

Doris grows up to be a witch, but it doesn't pay the bills, so
she becomes a housekeeper for a veteran of the Great War, a mil-
itary man gassed in the trenches. It's really the same story. Different costumes. Different season. Sweltering summer, suburban,
depression-seized London. Doris in her small room off the
kitchen. She unties her apron, lifts it off, unbuttons her blue dress
and drags it over her head. She sits on the cot in her slip, wipes
the sweat off her chest with the pads of her fingers, pulls the
cheap slip up her thigh to unclip her stockings from the garter
belt. The doorknob turns, the door opens. It is her employer,
fully dressed in khaki uniform. Doris smiles bewitchingly.

Out of this union, my father was born, a bastard in the classical
sense. Doris had two more children, daughters, with her employer,

and then their disorderly little domestic arrangement was interrupted by the greater disorder of World War Two. When Doris's daughter brought home a new boyfriend, an American sailor, the family alchemy prevailed. Doris seduced him away from her daughter and married him. (There are actually sixteen half brothers and sisters. My father has tried to sort them out for me, but I can't figure out how all these children were possible.)

My father never saw his father again. The man who was gassed at Somme married over and over, compulsively, died in his sixties, with at least thirteen children, on his sixth marriage, to a twenty-two-year-old woman. Beginning with my father, he named each firstborn son after himself, as if he could erase my father and start over and over.

Doris followed the American sailor home, died in Florida, ninety-six, sitting in her chair. In her will there was no mention of my father, though he says he called her once a week, on Sunday. My father says, She did not leave me a thing, not a pin, feather, book, no keepsake, as if I never existed.

In some moods, my father follows the family tradition of erasure. Sometimes he does not acknowledge his parents at all. He traces his true ancestry to the Celts. He idolizes Boadicea, Celtic warrior queen, shrieking magic incantations, bloodied sword held high, leading a rebellion against the Roman invaders. He called me just the other day, with directions for the preparation of his body after he dies. He claims to know the hour of his death, he inherited his mother's gifts, but only laughs when I ask him to reveal it. He wishes to be painted blue and bent into the lotus position before rigor mortis sets in. Like the Celts, my father's sacred color is blue.

The Celts had their long moment when most of Europe was theirs. They waded around in dank bogs under the white moon, wearing animal skins and sacrificing people to the gods. They built enormous bonfires. They loved gold, twisted into thick braids and worn around their necks. They melted into foxes and goats, then back again. They knew all there was to know about the properties of oak, mistletoe and heather. They respected druids, storytellers and warriors. No one else mattered much.

Then the Romans scoured them out, the Saxons rode over them, the British prevailed and eventually my father. But my father won't admit connection to the invaders. Part druid, part storyteller, part warrior, it's as if he rose out of that bog straight into the twentieth century, looking for the bonfire.

But my father is not simply a screaming pagan, he loves chivalry, too. When he was studying art at university he built a dragon. He asked every pretty girl on campus to duck under the green silk, lift the bamboo, make the dragon move in sinuous waves. Then he dressed himself in chain mail and slew it. He was a color-blind artist, his paintings inky Rorschachs. One day he grew frustrated with painting. He built all his art supplies into a pyre, threw gasoline on and burned everything. He quit art school. He decided he would either join the Royal Navy or emigrate to America and become a cowboy. He sent for a passport and the navy papers, both at once. The passport arrived first, and because my father never had any patience, or because he believed in fate and a fresh start, he ended up wearing jeans, cowboy boots and a work shirt and sitting in a bar somewhere in Nevada.

Supposedly, a man walks in and asks him if he can ride a horse. My father, who has never seen a horse except ones ridden by the London bobbies, says, You bet, Pardner, in his best John Wayne drawl. My father says he lied a lot and learned quickly. This turned out not to be his life's calling, however. It was time to disappear into the sunset. Because of his cowboy past, he got the job as farming instructor at a summer camp in the Catskills for disturbed children.

He hadn't realized it was a camp run by Jews. He'd only met one Jew in his whole life, a neighbor in his youth who played the violin. During World War Two this Jewish man had cried in their kitchen, wearing velvet slippers. Now, here was a whole camp full of the people who were at the heart of the very war that had defined my father's childhood. They all seemed exotic, sensitive, dark-haired, even the light-haired ones.

My father says, Your mother was the most beautiful, bright, intelligent being I had ever met. I fell in love on the instant. My father says my mother's only fault was that she thought she was George Washington and had never told a lie.

My mother is more cagey. She says she liked him a lot. She says he told wild stories, and she never believed a word he said. She says, A lot of it turned out to be true, but since you couldn't tell which was which, it was probably advisable not to believe any of it. She doesn't mention whether it mattered to her that at twenty-one, he had already been married and divorced, or that there were razor-thin white scars on both his wrists.

What did my father do to show his love for my mother?

Recite poetry, read her *Winnie the Pooh* when she came down with the flu, give her a small white vase, ask her to marry him. My mother thought he was romantic and amusing but would make an unreliable husband. Have I mentioned how skinny my father was? Painfully so, and pale, with buck-teeth. He was a hypodermic needle filled with passion.

They left the Catskills and returned to New York, both of them, but not together. They remained friends, their relationship cemented by my father's unrequited lust. He hung around, helped paint my grandparents' house for them, played old blues albums for my mother, gave her a turquoise mohair blanket. Once, he was walking in Central Park with my grandfather and stopped in what seemed like a random swatch of woods. He dug in the dirt and unburied a set of dishes, told my grandfather he had left them there in case of need.

But my mother felt the need to marry. If one wasn't engaged by senior year in college, one might get stuck forever in one's parents' house in Brooklyn. She went on a blind date with a tall, Jewish medical student who grew African violets on his fire escape and liked the zoo.

My mother decided to marry the medical student. As my father sat at the wedding of my mother, he swore someday she would be his. There are photos of him sitting at the wedding, thinking this. He looks like the wild card—his legs jauntily crossed into the aisle, his Rasputin goatee, his smirk. Have I mentioned that he bore a startling resemblance to Abraham Lincoln?

My mother wore a small veil that just grazed her chin and a white ankle-length dress with a hoop skirt. She had a twenty-one-inch waist.

She and the medical student spent their honeymoon at my father's rented house in the country. My father took this medical student on a hike. He led him up a mountain and left him there. The medical student eventually thrashed his way down the mountain. My father married a British nurse. My mother was the maid of honor at my father's wedding. My father and his nurse moved back to England, and for a while, at least to my mother, this seemed like the end of the story.

When perturbed, my mother's medical student gave her a few days' silent treatment. When working at home, he locked the door to his office and whispered into his tape recorder. When not working or going to school, my mother sat in a tree by the house, studying for her Ph.D. in special ed. They went to their Italian neighbors for dinner each Friday night. There, the heavy tomato sauce seemed to put my mother in a trance, and she would fall into a drugged sleep on the couch. A year and a half after the wedding, during one three-day silent treatment, my mother plotted her escape.

It was the sixties now, so she got a Mexican divorce and rode around New York on a motor scooter, dating three different men at once. She began wearing violently colored minidresses.

She was twenty-four, sexy, kind, had a blackened tooth. She was restless, she wanted a better world, she wanted true love. If she had an anthem, it would have been, No more locked doors, forever. My mother decided to go to Europe by herself. She walked into a travel agency, but when she began to ask for the ticket she went into a coughing fit. You've never heard my mother cough. It always startles, coming from such a small, neat personage. It's her shout, her yawp, her howl. She had to leave the travel agency minus the ticket. She tried again—same coughing fit. Maybe some part of her knew where this trip would lead. Finally, she bought the ticket over the phone. She met my father in England. He said he had separated from his nurse. He asked my mother to marry him again. She said she'd think about it.

My mother went to Switzerland and climbed an alp. She stood up there in the thin air that makes your brain woozy, at the beginning of a fresh new decade, and thought, If I marry him, my life will be full of surprises. She decided to take a chance.

They met in Paris. My mother had acquired new black French underwear for the occasion. My father was so emaciated, he would have dizzy spells and have to lie down on the sidewalk. His love had been simmering for six years. They procured a room in a little pension. My mother climbed the stairs, aware of my father's body behind her, aware of the new bra biting into her ribs. My father staggered behind. I imagine the hotel shaking from the minor volcano of their consummation, a small trail of lava flowing under their bedroom door.

Later, there was a rap on that door, the concierge informed my father that his wife was waiting below. She had hired a detective to follow my father, as they actually were not separated after all. Still, my mother returned from Europe, pregnant with me.

When my father finally got a divorce and a visa and joined my mother in the States, my just-married parents moved into my grandparents' attic in Brooklyn. My father painted Scottish dancing men in kilts and peacocks on the walls. Sometimes they would meet on the steep attic stairs, one going up, one going down. They would start to talk, sit down on the steps, and it would be hours.

We have this home movie that my father and grandfather and mother made around this time. Dad plays the bad cowboy, dressed in black, my grandfather the good cowboy in a giant white Stetson. Dad tries to steal the pretty young thing, played by my mother, but Grandpa shoots him down and rescues the girl. This mime of present and future tension is acted out in silence, and might seem ominous, except for the fact that it is clear they are all having a ball, their teeth gritted from holding back laughter.

While my mother was pregnant, my father looked for work. Then as now, he gravitated towards frenzied get-rich-quick schemes or professions in which he could wear a costume. He took a job as a butcher, spent the little money they had on a heavy white apron and big boots so he could wade through entrails. He quit after a day, bored or disinclined. Then, instead of searching for work, he went to double matinees.

While I incubated, they made a plan for their future. They would start a school for disturbed adolescents. My mother typed up brochures that vaguely described a charming rural school, a school they could not begin until they had some tuition money. They had to wait weeks to send out the brochures because they couldn't afford the stamps.

My father wanted to name me Boadicea, but my mother nixed that. They compromised and named me after a male prophet in the Bible, but deliberately mispronounced it, so that their little girl would be, like all the rest of their plans, a reinvention.

President Kennedy was shot. JFK Junior said he didn't remember his father's death, he was too young, or the past had been obliterated by the photograph of his salute, but my mother remembers, maybe your mother remembers, too. She was standing at the kitchen sink, doing dishes, listening to the radio. The announcer's voice cracked, and it could have been her own. She remembers the feel of the warm water pouring off her hands. All the Jews at one end of East Ninth Street wept, and the Catholics at the other end wept, too.

My parents bought five hundred and fifty acres of land in the Adirondack Mountains with twenty thousand dollars they borrowed from one of my mother's old boyfriends. Friends and troubled teenagers were going to gather together to make a saner, sweeter world. They grabbed me up, six weeks old, and escaped the city in their decrepit Land Rover.

I can picture them on that long six-hour ride from New York City, driving over the edge of the world, surrounded by trees, ready for everything. November, the jeep cold enough that their breath smoked. Bouncing over the back roads, maybe they kissed over my bald baby head, my father's tongue in my mother's mouth, my father's staccato laugh, my mother's wide smile with the discolored tooth, me between them like a good luck charm.

CHAPTER EIGHT

happily ever after

Summer 1973

AFTER the Celtic and Roman battle, after The Rift, as it came to be known in the valley, after the camping trip and the students return to their homes for summer vacation, my family travels to England. I learn later that the trip is carefully constructed, my father's effort to erase Paul, to remind my mother that, after the whole spool of thread has unraveled, we can still wind it back again. We are still a nuclear family.

But all I know is that we are finally going to the land of stories. Not just Narnia and Alice and King Arthur and Boadicea, but Crazy Harmon and World War Two. Now my father's eccentricity will be explained.

We sail to England on the *France,* the longest cruise ship in the world. (I have no idea where this money came from.) Our stateroom is covered over in blue velvet. There is a magician on board, and movie theaters. We all watch *Fiddler on the Roof* three times, and we all cry three times.

When we arrive in England, the people at customs keep mistaking Dad for a Yank. And it's true, their accents are different than his. My father doesn't think this is funny. He is grim, humiliated. As we walk out of customs, none of us dares to talk to him, not until he has regained his Englishness. Within the day, his accent increases until he's found the proper authentic inflection. I begin to think that England might not explain my father after all.

We rent a cottage in Devon. Primavera Cottage reminds me of Snow White and Rose Red. It has a half acre of manicured rose gardens, and roses climb up its white walls. The ceilings are low because, my father says, people were shorter back then. I ask Dad if the house is really, really old. He says, Oh, yes, George Washington slept here. I wonder which bed.

We are given a kitten each, we play Barbie dolls amongst the roses. We watch *Little Women* on the BBC. My mother tells me television is better in England, and I figure that means they get more channels. My parents watch a show that takes place in a public bathroom in a subway station. They laugh together.

We walk to an inn on a little green trail through the fields and eat veal with ham and cheese in the middle. We eat meat pasties, fish and chips and scones with Devonshire cream.

England is not the grand land of chaos and war I had expected. It's sweet and safe, it's like the secret garden in the book. I want to be a little British girl and never go home. We are given leather school satchels, though we will never be here long enough to go to school. My father buys me a green flowered cotton smock dress like the ones I've seen on the girls in the village, and I wear it every day.

My father's half brother comes to visit. His brother shares the same first name as my father. My father's brother plays the violin in a symphony orchestra. He gives my father some kind of card certifying he is a violinist in the symphony orchestra. This delights my father.

My father's teacher from art school and his wife come to visit. His teacher's wife has thick hair that reaches her ankles. While she suns in her bikini underwear in the rose garden, she lets down her golden hair, and we comb it out. A few weeks later, we visit them in London. In his teacher's apartment, there is a room for owls. The room is dark, and when you open the door you can make out wooden perches and glowing eyes, the sound of fluttering. The teacher keeps owls for observation, because he is trying to become a bird. He shows us a film of his trial flight runs. He has constructed giant feathery wings and is being pulled along on a gurney. He flaps his wings in large, sweeping motions.

It doesn't work. Yet, he adds cheerfully.

In England, Icarus would not have fallen. In England, transformation is painless, delightful, as easy as a slow-motion film of a rose in bloom. England is the land of the garden, rather than the forest. A British garden is everything the dark Adirondack forest is not: pruned, well tended, tamed. Beside an English garden, there is always a little cottage that holds an industrious woodcutter and his wife, who long for a child, and will soon grow or find one. A shack in the Adirondack forest holds a dirty hermit dressed in deerskin and feathers, cursing God.

There are green fields, moors where small, shaggy ponies crowd our car; Jo March refuses to marry Laurie, spoiling the happy ending of *Little Women,* but my mother promises Jo will marry a nice man in a future book; there are lupines, foxgloves, hedgerows. We visit a ruined castle that my father tells me is Camelot.

My mother spends much of her time embroidering. She sits on a blanket in the rose garden. She embroiders a woman in a Victorian dress sitting in a rose garden. But what is she thinking? Why do we have to tug at her chin and call her name to bring her back to us? Is it the small, thick hands? The big, white teeth? Is it his singing voice, deep and slow as molasses?

Do you know the old, English story "The Nightingale"? A man and woman are neighbors, two stone castles pressed next to each other in a crowded town. When the woman's husband is asleep, she unlatches the leaded window, paned with thick, bubbled glass. It hasn't been opened in so long, and she has to dig her nails into the rotting wood, pry it open. Her neighbor does the same on his side, and they talk.

Finally, the husband asks his wife why she stands at the window so often, and she replies, To listen to the voice of the nightingale.

The husband takes care of that. He kills a nightingale, plucks its feathers, serves it to his wife like pheasant under glass. He laughs angrily. No more reason to go to the window, my dear. Now, she sits demurely, embroidering, hundreds of little stitches called lovers' knots, and she does not hear her husband or her daughters calling to her, because the window has been opened, and there's no shutting it now.

CHAPTER NINE

the new mother

1973–1974

WHEN WE RETURN from England in September, I am taken to the dentist. I hear my mother tell someone that the dentist is a Holocaust survivor. I think this means he's a Nazi. When the old man with the stiff accent enters the room, I go hysterical. We have to leave without the examination. We try another dentist. This exam goes off without trauma. Afterwards, my mother explains to me that I have my father's teeth crammed into her tiny mouth. The dentist will have to remove some of my big teeth, to make room for the others. Eleven of them.

They put a mask on my mouth, tell me to count backwards from ten. The dentist and technicians begin to turn to putty, their faces and voices stretching. Then I fall down the dark hole in my nighttime visions. I can't stop myself. I wake crying, surrounded by blood, wide-open spaces cleared in my jaw.

We are at the Little School, which is much littler this fall. My father appears one afternoon, with a paper sack of penny candy. He hands it off to Bo, saying, Share. Then he gets back into the MG and is off to wherever he is off to. We put our hands out to Bo, but he grins, turns and takes off with the candy. We all give chase. I can't believe it, but I'm gaining on him. I reach out, touch his sandy hair. My fist closes around it and, without knowing exactly what I'm doing, I yank. Bo hurtles backwards. He lands hard on his back. The candy sprays out of the bag. Dustin and Beky scramble to pick the Tootsie Rolls and Smarties out of the grass, but Bo and I stare at each other.

Then he tackles me.

He throws me on my stomach and lands heavily on my back. I'm yelling and struggling. He hooks a finger into each side of my mouth and begins to pull. I fear that my lips will tear. His mother, Ellen, comes out on the steps of the Little School. He leaps off of me and runs.

I am hysterical. Bo climbs onto the roof of the trailer and refuses to come down. I think he should be caned, maybe executed. But Ellen doesn't get involved, and eventually we find our way back to each other.

A few weeks later, my mother tells me Bo, Dustin and Ellen are moving to Maine to live with Ellen's new, rich boyfriend. Ellen lets Bo drive the car down the dirt road when they leave.

Except for a visit every few years, Bo and I will grow up without each other. He will transform into a six-foot-five bachelor addicted to physical risk. During the week he will work as a reading specialist, during the weekend he will ice climb until he hurts himself. Once, he will try to tell his mother and Dustin about what happened in the barn, but they won't want to know. He will sleep with a loaded gun by his bed every night.

Kitty finally pulls out one clump of hair too many. She calls Laurie, her housemother, a white bitch and yanks out a fist of hair. The staff decides Kitty has to go back to reform school. Kitty does not leave me any mementos, not her Jackson Five album, her pick or a gold chain. On the day she has to leave, Kitty sits on my mother's lap. Their arms around each other, they both cry.

Doug leaves soon after. He spends the rest of the fall picking apples in Vermont, then drifts back to White Plains. A few months later, he calls late one night. He is addicted to heroin again. My mother talks him into going to a detox center in Vermont. After the second week of detox, we are allowed to visit him.

My mother, Angie, my sister and I meet him in the cafeteria of the center: long wooden folding tables and metal folding chairs, lines of candy, soda and cigarette machines along the wall, the smell of strong disinfectant. Bearded men play cards in one corner. Doug wears a green flannel shirt. He has turned puffy, everywhere except his legs and butt, and he continually hitches up his jeans.

We used to tease him about this, calling him Mooner, but this place makes Beky and me shy, and we stand quietly, holding on to the back of my mother's chair. Angie smiles down at her knees. Doug crosses his legs, smokes the cigarettes we bought him out of the machine, talks fast. There are dark, tender places under his eyes, and his skin looks see-through. He hums song lyrics under his breath, laughs, doesn't look at Angie. He cracks some old jokes, then says, Jeez, you girls are all grown up, as if he doesn't know what to do with us.

Beky and I are relieved to leave the center, so is Angie.

Doug stays in Vermont after the detox program. He tells us he has a new girlfriend. I'm glad he's not alone, my mother says.

I become obsessed with a children's book called *Gertrude's Child*. Gertrude is a doll who runs away from her little girl. She walks stiffly through the rain and lets the drops slide off her face without wiping them away. She walks alone through the night and is not afraid. She is made of wood and doesn't care. Gertrude is my hero.

After a night alone in the rain, Gertrude comes to a shop that sells real children. She buys a droopy girl named Annie. Annie lets Gertrude undress her in the snow; she lets Gertrude snip off all her golden curls until she's bald. Gertrude leaves her in the tub, and Annie doesn't even try to get out. She just sags there all night and catches a cold.

This pathetic Annie sends me into paroxysms. I grind my teeth, roll on the floor, clench my fists. I want to squeeze her and squeeze her. I am happy when a lion almost eats Annie. I can feel my sharp teeth cracking her bones. I am proud of Gertrude for pouring hot tea on the lion and saving the little girl, then vaguely disappointed at the end when the doll and the girl become friends, and Gertrude's wooden heart begins to throb painfully with feeling.

I have my chance to play Gertrude when a new child named Alfie arrives. He must have been very small, or perhaps troubled: he can hardly talk. I don't know what he is doing here, but he clearly doesn't like it. He spends all his time standing in the mud-room in front of the long windows on each side of the Little School's door, crying. Tears and snot run down his pale face. I am outraged that no one comforts him. I am outraged at the whining noises he makes and at the leaking tears, his square haircut and neatly collared shirt.

I sneak out to the mudroom and torment him. I whisper through clenched teeth, I'm going to get you. I chase him around the room, playing Gertrude with stiff-legged steps, my eyes painted into slits. Or I become the lion, growl, Stop crying or I'm going to eat you. I hate the tears and snot on his face, evidence of his grief. I don't share this game with Beky. I don't tell anyone.

Usually Alfie just presses his hot face against the glass and ignores me, but one day he runs into the classroom for help. He tries to explain through his gasping sobs, but he can't talk well enough to describe how I torture him. He gives up trying and just points at me. I widen my eyes, play innocent. Shrug. The teacher of the day doesn't get it.

One day he is no longer there. I don't remember any explanations.

*

I decide to write a book. I fold sheets of pink construction paper in half and staple the binding, but before I can begin composing, my mother says it's time for bed. I haven't even started the story, but up I go. As soon as my mother leaves I pull my blank book out from under the pillow. I drag the lamp over towards my bed, as far as the cord will stretch. Then, very cleverly and sneakily, I take out my best taffeta dress and drape it over the bulb. I turn on the lamp. The light shines greenly through the dress. It's pretty, like a stained-glass window, and not bright enough for my mother to detect from downstairs. I take up my pen and begin to write.

About fifteen minutes later I walk cautiously down the stairs. Mom?

She looks up from the paperwork she is doing at the dining room table. You're supposed to be asleep.

Can I talk to you?

In the morning, Honey.

But it's important.

She lets me sit down next to her.

What is it?

Well—

Just tell me.

It's just that . . .

Tell me.

The house is on fire.

With a screech my mother dashes up the stairs. She comes running down, holding the burning lamp. The dress is stuck to the bulb and in flames, so is the shade. The cord whips behind her like an angry tail. She throws the whole thing in our deep kitchen sink and turns the faucet on. Smoke roils up, the smell is awful. My dress is black and sticky-looking.

My mother gently explains the causal relationship between light, heat and fire. She doesn't explain how writing fits in.

In winter, the main house burns down. No one is hurt, but the meeting house, the cafeteria, the office, students' bedrooms, all gone.

In the spring, Paul and my mother drive Laurie to the hospital, where she has a baby girl. Beky and I are the only children our age left in the valley. My father buys us old ballerina costumes, all glittery with sequins. Beky's is pale blue, mine black. We perform songs in these outfits, "Won't You Come Home Bill Bailey" and "Billy Don't Be a Hero." Neither of us knows how to snap our fingers, but we click our tongues, press our fingers together and pretend.

It's spring 1973, and the women are fed up. They want their own Royal Navy trip. My father is amenable. He will take all the women out on Lake Champlain. My father says he is a great supporter of women's liberation. He says he can't wait until the time when the women are seducing him.

My mother declines to go, and we're not invited either. But this is the last Royal Navy trip, so don't miss it. My father lets a female teacher drive the van, makes a show of sitting in the way back, his arms around two young women. You giggle and shriek and sing dirty Royal Navy songs my father teaches you. When you get out on the water and begin rowing and drinking the required rum, the sun is hot, so you all decide to take your shirts off. Twelve bare-breasted rowers and my father their commander, drunk and meandering on the flat green waters of Lake Champlain, the Adirondacks on one side, the Green Mountains on the other. Fishermen and ferryboat tourists stare, shade their eyes, pick up their binoculars. A new day has dawned.

You all stumble off the boat at the end of the day, sunburned and stomachs curdling. My father disappears in the bushes with a drunk female student, it won't take long. On the way home he stops off at a hotel with a female teacher and arrives in time for dinner.

My mother has already heard all about it. She's not amused. That night, they have one of their fights, and my father slams out of the house and disappears. All night long, my mother thinks, Accident. In the morning she finds out he spent the night in the basement on a cot.

My mother and father's fights have grown louder and more frequent. My mother makes dinner. My father does not show up. My mother's cheerfulness is exactly equal to a tense silence. Then my father arrives, impossibly late, blustery, always with a gift. The fight begins. My mother's voice, accusing. My father's harassed. The first crash when my father throws something, the second crash of the door as he slams out, and then the gasping sound of my mother crying.

My sister and I peek around the stone fireplace, watch them until we can't stand it anymore, then rush over to their bed and jump on, rolling around in fits of hysterical laughter.

I ask my mother if they are going to get a divorce. Not in a thousand years, she says.

My mother has to go to a meeting in New York City. She says Dad will take care of us. As soon as she leaves, Dad says Angie, Doug's old girlfriend, is going to be our baby-sitter. That first evening I like having a baby-sitter. Angie helps us bake her specialty, dream bars. They taste great. And Angie is pretty and nice. But then at night, she doesn't leave. She sleeps with my father.

The next day the four of us go into town. My father walks ahead of us, holding hands with Angie. Dad asks her if she likes being a mother. They both laugh. I want to say something about Mom, just to invoke her name, but I can't think of what to say. I feel dizzy, as if the world has tilted and swept us off into somewhere else, and I am the only one who has noticed.

At night, I can't sleep. The mice are driving me crazy. I lie down on the floor beside my sister's bed and cry without any sound. I don't want to scare her. She doesn't seem to notice the scratching in the walls.

Finally, my real mother calls. I watch my father tell her everything is fine. Then he hands the phone to me. My father stands behind me. The cord is stretched over my shoulder, pressing against my neck. She asks how we are. It is hard to breathe. I say the words I know will crack through this game my father's playing, if it is a game.

Is Angie our mother now?

My mother comes home. She and my father want to be alone in the cabin. Laurie takes us to her A-frame to bake a cake. While we measure flour I look out the window. Dad's MG speeds down the road, spraying gravel. I see the backs of my mother and father's identical dark brown hair. They're leaving us, I say, gripping the windowsill. Laurie stands behind me. That's not your mother, she says. That's Angie.

CHAPTER TEN

i'm rubber, you're glue

1974

WHILE WE BAKE that cake with Laurie in the A-frame, our family breaks open in the log cabin. We pour the mix into the tin bowl. My parents are screaming about lies, infidelity, money, neither remembers the words. Only the pitch remains. We add a quarter cup of oil. For the first time, my mother is the one who begins throwing dishes, antique plates with a green filigree design.

Beky and I beat with an electric mixer.

My mother is smashing every dish in the house now. My mother says this smashing breaks a spell, as if she is some bewitched princess waking from a long sleep. Maybe it's the moment she wakes up and joins the women's liberation movement. My father is standing at the door. He says this is the point at which my mother lifts up the heavy iron Buddha that stands on the mantel and heaves it at him, marking his fate. Rinpoche, my father's future Buddhist teacher, will say later that if the statue had hit him, my father would have become instantly enlightened. But the Buddha smashes against the wall, and my father has a long way to go.

Beky and I lick the beaters, run our fingers over the bowl.

My father skitters his MG backwards down the hill, meets Angie halfway down as she is climbing up barefoot.

I look out the window and watch the MG speed off. I am still holding the beater. Laurie takes us up to the cabin. My mother is lying in her bed, sobbing so hard she can't speak. Her face is red. The pillow and covers are damp with her tears. We climb up, one on each side of her. She tells us that she and Dad are separating. A trial separation for six weeks. My sister and I begin to cry, too.

I want my daddy, Beky cries.

I think about the dark back of his head, not even a backwards glance or a wave as he drives away. I hate him, I say.

He buys Angie shoes when they reach Montreal. I know this because my mother receives the bill from the credit card company. My mother calls Angie's parents. Angie's mother says she is not surprised. Angie has tried to seduce her own stepfather. It isn't like that, my mother answers, but she doesn't explain further.

After buying clothes in Montreal, Angie and my father make their way to Maine, where he keeps his boat, the *Blue Nose Two*, bought with the insurance money from the main house fire. We spent a week on the boat once. I know that drive through Maine, the grey road, the miles of dense evergreen. No houses. I remember lying in the back of the car in the bed that my mother made for us, the cocoon feeling, drifting in and out of sleep, my parents' voices as we cruised through the night.

On the boat I read British mysteries by Enid Blyton about children who sailed to a secret island, but when my father wanted to sail us to a real island, I panicked, thinking of my father maneuvering us through pitching waves. He agreed to stay in the harbor. He bought Beky and me silver lockets. My mother glued tiny oval pictures into the locket, one of her, one of him.

Angie is only six years older than I am. I don't know if she is given a silver locket, but three weeks later, my father rows Angie ashore and leaves her there. I can imagine Angie, standing on a wooded and rocky coast, her long hair whipping around. I can picture the shoes she bought, red platforms that make her list dangerously on the rocks. I cannot picture her wailing, although I would have wailed, pitched rocks at the departing dinghy. I cannot even picture her angry. My memory of Angie is only of beauty. In the failure of my imagination, Angie is calm as the Buddha as she makes her way into the rest of her life.

My father is ready to come home.

Too late. My mother, knee-deep in tears, is grieving the end of their relationship. All those clichés about tears make sense to me when I think of my mother that spring and summer—buckets, rivers and lakes.

A few weeks later, we have our first weekend visit with him. He picks us up at the valley in his new, white Opal GT. I had always thought of him as fashioned for the grand gesture, his mind set on conquest, and I am unused to the particularity of his attention. I make brittle conversation. So Dad, what have you been up to? Beky sits next to me and says nothing. She is a quiet child in general, in fact, our play together is often without words, but now she has grown beyond quiet into silent. She will hardly speak for the next two or three years.

As we speed along, he tells us it is Father's Day. We sit in the cramped backseat, ashamed that we have no present for the admiral of extravagant gifts, and no money to buy one. He pulls over in front of a men's clothing store and sends us in with a twenty to buy him underwear.

We open the jangling door and are confronted with rows of men's clothes. Under the smirking eye of the clerk in his tweedy suit, we pick out some red and blue men's bikinis. Dad has told us medium, but the clerk reads off mysterious numbers we don't know how to interpret. Unable to deliver even this sham gift, we walk down the steps of the store empty-handed. He goes in and buys himself the underwear. He and the clerk laugh together, while Beky and I hang behind him.

Later, we stand in the Howard Johnson's hotel parking lot and watch as he paints an oval British flag on the hood of his car. He uses masking tape so that the stripes are flawless. As always, I admire his lack of hesitation. But his canvas has shrunk from the whole valley to the hood of his sports car. I don't like to see him readying his little caravan, cast out to wander. He is alone, a bright Lucifer father, falling away from us.

I am wrong in this. He is leaving us, but he is not alone. I don't know it then, but at a dharma center in Vermont a few weeks earlier, he has already met the second great love of his life, a Tibetan Buddhist teacher, a monk who has fled over the mountains of Tibet, been educated at Oxford, been crippled in an automobile accident. At this retreat in Vermont, my father sat in the audience, watching the students closest to Rinpoche plump their teacher's seat cushions and hand him cold glasses of water. Electric with desire, my father hated those students, vowed someday to become the shadow behind Rinpoche's chair.

Meanwhile, I have my own ambitions.

I walk up to my mother who has been crying for days in their antique four-poster bed. Her sobs scrape my ears. Her thin shoulders shake. Occasionally, she wipes her red nose with an edge of the blue and red brocade bedspread.

I stand by the bed, say, I'm not going to sit around all summer and watch you have a nervous breakdown. I open my fist and hand her a crumpled pamphlet I found amongst the stacks of mail: glossy girls around a campfire, arms entwined, mouths rounded in song.

Six weeks later I am on my way to Quaker summer camp, paid for by scholarship. My mother and I cross into Vermont, the car windows down.

I say, Are you and Dad ever getting back together?

She says, No.

I say, Why do you hate him?

I don't remember her words, probably something like, I don't hate him, I just don't trust him, because he lies. But what I hear is that my father has fallen into league with the others, the ones who are not us, the unchosen ones who are responsible for the Holocaust and for the war in Vietnam. The ones who can't be trusted. Because they lie.

I hate that, too, I say, watching the green fields with their black-and-white cows.

Camp Little Flower looks as dark and dirty as our log cabin, and this is comforting—dark and dirty is familiar decor. There is a compost heap, pig slop in white plastic buckets, chickens squawking; porcupines have gnawed holes in the side of our lean-to, a lean-to that already smells of mildewed towels. My Newberry's tin trunk is pushed under my bed.

My mother kisses me, promises to write every day, her eyes tear up and she disappears from the doorway. I unroll my sleeping bag on a wooden bunk already claimed by generations of girlish signatures. Polly was here, 1960, Erica loves Alan, 1966. Kate, Gigi. I know none of these names. Homesickness fills my heart, but not for the home as it is now. I find myself missing Laura Ingalls Wilder's log cabin instead of my own.

Soon it is blue evening and there are a dozen ten-year-old girls around the fire, coughing on smoke, our faces strange to each other. I have never been amongst so many girls my own age, never amongst so many unknown faces. For courage, I think of my current hero, Mary Jemison, Indian Captive. She was stolen away from everything she knew, but by the end of the story you couldn't tell the difference between her and a real Iroquois woman.

We roast doughboys, globs of Bisquick stuck on a stick. The skinny sticks we scrounge from the woods sag with their doughy load. We grip the sticks with two hands, our fingers and palms stiff from dried Bisquick. Some, like me, hold the doughboy too close and it flames, others toast it to a fine brown. The girl next to me loses her blob to the fire. Her voice trembles. My knee brushes hers. She flinches away. I can see other fires, with other circles of girls, their backs turned against me.

The counselors say we are going to play a game to get to know each other. Their voices bright: Everyone must think of three things about themselves. Two will be true, one a lie. Then we will try to figure out which is which.

I groan with the rest, my heart racing. The circle grows quiet as we all begin desperate invention. Here is a game that could help me gain friends. There are truths I discard immediately — principally the fact that I might be the sole survivor of a major shipwreck. I think of truths that might attract interest: my father plays at war, we own shaggy orange cows, I lived in a teepee.

For lies to work they need to sound ordinary. I know what is ordinary because I play with Barbie dolls: I have a little sister named Skipper, I have a friend named Ken, I live in a dream house.

We go round the circle, girls are laughing and eager, and not very good at this game. Some tell more than one lie, while others don't know how to handle falsehood: they giggle, look sideways, twitch their mouths, pause or keep the lie for the end. Their lies are extravagant and obvious.

My turn. Number one, I have a friend named Ken. No reaction. I hurry on to the good part. Number two, my father likes to play war, so we divide the whole school up into two groups, like Celtics and Romans. People are wearing grain sacks, they're supposed to be loincloths I guess.

I look around at the Quaker girls' faces. They think I'm an insane warmonger. But I chatter on. I can't help myself. I have never been taught how to talk to strangers.

And one side stays at home, and the other side hides in the woods and puts barbed wire all around their camp. Then we have these battles with firecrackers and water balloons and big buckets of cow manure and it's crazy, everyone yelling and people have cow manure running down their faces, and the last time they got so carried away they burned down the bell tower.

I get a few nervous snickers. I breathe, swallow, try something simple. Number three, I live on a commune.

What's a commune? one whispers. The girl next to her shrugs, rolls her eyes. There is an anxious silence.

And here is the rub. After I've told too much, too late, I see how the truth will outcast me. But I have an escape plan. It is my turn to reveal: The truth is I have a friend named Ken. Everything else is a lie.

I wonder if, hundreds of miles away, my mother can feel the rupture. I will never be all right again. I have taken up lying. I have joined Lilith. I am in secret league with the devil.

Speaking of, one Saturday my father shows up for a visit. It's just us, on a green hill in a cow pasture above the camp. He's brought a picnic, soda and chips and candy, all the contraband that's not allowed at my health food camp.

I slug Mountain Dew. Try nervously to entertain. You know what, Dad? We always know when to do something, because there are bells that ring for beading or meals or swimming. And at swimming we have something called the fifth freedom. We don't have to wear clothes. We never have to wear clothes if we don't want to.

And I have two best friends, their names are Hope and Gretchen. And there's this girl we can't stand, she's always saying mean things to us, but we just say, I know you are, but what am I, or we say, I'm rubber, you're glue, whatever you say bounces off me and sticks to you.

He tells me he's following his guru out west, we won't see each other for a while.

And I've only been homesick one time. We went on an overnight, and I had to have my sleeping bag on the outside by the opening. But the counselor let me sleep with her. (I was silent until I exploded in tears. The counselor pulled me out of my sleeping bag and popped me into hers. She was naked, and the shock of heat and skin stopped my sobs. I slept all night in the comforting sauna of her arms.)

How do you feel about me and your mom separating?

I'm glad you and Mom are separated, I say brightly, because I can spend time with you alone.

Even though I won't be seeing you, if you ever need anything . . . he says.

I am giddy with caffeinated soda and candy, and the conversation is going so well. Know what, Dad? I always thought you liked Beky best.

I do, he says. Micah, did you know that my mother foretold I would have two blond daughters, and one of them would be a lesbian. Have you ever thought you might be a lesbian?

Dad!

With those thick ankles. Poor girl, you got those from me. I've always thought of you as very masculine. I've always thought of Beky as my daughter and you as a friend.

The dross crackles away and I'm left with a hard, silver smirk. I have enough friends, I say.

He laughs.

My mother writes me every day:

— *I love you, Darling.*

— *We are closing the school, we'll have a final ceremony on the hill.* (Everyone drifts off into the seventies. Ann will become a lawyer, Kitty a social worker, Giovanni a born-again Christian.)

— *I've gotten a job at a counseling service in a little town in Vermont. You can go to school there, with lots of kids your own age.* (Imagine me with a striped ribbon in my ponytail, a heart-patterned turtleneck, chinos and clogs. I play field hockey, I am school spirited. In the privacy of my own room I either read historical fiction or put on Paul Anka's "She's Having My Baby" and dance around in a green leotard.)

— *Beky and I have picked out an apartment, it's on a cute lane. You'll love it. You can choose the wallpaper for your room. Doug has moved back to White Plains, but he may come live with us in Vermont in the fall. He'll be like a foster brother for you.*

— *We miss you, we're counting the days until we see you again.*

— *Darling, Laurie and Paul have decided to separate. Laurie and the baby are moving to Boston, she's going back to school.*

Paul is going to stay with us. (I can imagine Laurie's wilted face when Paul tells her he is leaving her. She will become a professor and not remarry for eighteen years. She will hate my mother.)

—*I'm finally dealing with Beky's hair. Every day we sit and work on that knot. It's a whole month's project. She's so brave and patient! She doesn't even cry!*

—*Honey, I have something very, very sad to tell you. Doug has died. He died of a drug overdose. We're going to put a big stone in the garden behind the log cabin, to remember him.* (I ask my college-age counselor how you die of a drug overdose. She answers, It's not that hard.)

—*Just one more week and we'll be seeing you, we can't wait! We're counting the days!*

The last night of camp is Spy Night. There are twenty spies, chosen secretly. The rest of the hundred and fifty campers and counselors become guards, spreading out in rings around the main lodge, which for this one night, becomes the palace. The spies have to leave camp property and meet their chosen contact. With the contact's help, the spy then tries to break through enemy lines and into the palace without getting caught.

It's raining lightly. I hold the tiny slip of paper with the word spy scrawled on it that was passed to me an hour ago. I am in the woods with my contact, one of my best friends, just off camp property. (Twenty-five years later, I still remember the slight smattering of freckles and fine blond hair, the way she cocked her hip when restless, the slight sting as her palms hit mine in complicated clapping games.)

We have a plan. I pull off my shirt, pull down my shorts and underwear. I'm just wearing my sneakers now. My contact takes my clothes and puts them in the crook of a tree. Then she takes out the tub of lard we have stolen from the kitchen. I scoop out a palmful, splat it on my leg and begin to spread it. She takes another scoop and does my back. We are whispering, Shh. Will you shut up? and laughing through our noses and gritted teeth. I spread this lard everywhere, arms, torso, face, neck, legs. Then, we crouch down and wait.

It grows dark in the woods, and the lard seems to be attracting mosquitoes. We hear the bell that signals the beginning of the game. I have an hour to make it in. I can hear yelling. I'm jittery, and I don't want to wait any longer. Let's go, I say.

We begin to move through the woods, miming tigers stalking until it cracks us up and we just tiptoe. The first cabin is up ahead. We hide behind it. I peek out and see girls and women in ponchos with flashlights, calling excitedly to each other. There's a narrow, rock-strewn path that leads up a hill to the shining lights of the main lodge.

My friend says, Ready?

I nod.

She crashes through the woods, the guards take off after her and the path to the palace is empty. I start to run.

There's another one. This is a decoy. Get her! Get her! I can hear their feet pounding after me. I try to run faster, as fast as I've ever run. My chest hurts. Someone's barreling down the path towards me. I keep going.

She slips on the wet mud and falls. I'm hurt! she says.

I leap over her.

If you want to know the truth, I feel lion-like, feral, ready to use my teeth to escape, to reach the palace doors. I'm charging up the hill. I'm on the main lawn, sprinting across the wet grass. Palace guards are descending on me from all sides. One grabs my arm. Her hand slides down to my wrist. I shake her off and keep going. Another grabs at my back and screeches at the feel, recoils.

I have gotten away. No one will ever catch me.

I burst through the doors and stand panting in the light. The guards come in, laughing. My contact arrives, twigs in her hair. Everyone is shaking their heads, dabbing at the lard with their fingers. They cover me with a blanket, hand me a plastic cup of scalding, watery hot cocoa. The people that I was escaping from are the same people that I was escaping to. We hear someone yelling, Spy, Spy, the guards run back outside, and the game continues.

CHAPTER ELEVEN

do not cling

WHEN I ASK my mother if I can tape-record her for a memoir, she says, If I'm going to be betrayed it might as well be by my own daughter.

When I turn the tape on she chats for two hours about her childhood, her early relationship with my father, but she will not say anything on tape about the school, except this: There are things that your father did at the valley which I've always been ashamed of, which is probably why I don't want to talk about it. I guess I have fears about the world knowing that I was, in a way, an accomplice.

But before I tried to tape-record her, my mother liked to tell me secrets. Often, we are driving, to the dentist, to a college interview, my mother's hands at ten and two on the wheel, her deep voice filling the car full of stories I'm not sure I want to hear. Afterwards, I have the urge to roll the window down a turn and let the words rush out. But it is always too late. My mother's memory magically knots tight to my own, an endless pull of stained handkerchiefs.

I can see my father climbing the cement-block steps to the trailer that became the school office after the main house burnt down. He opens up the green book of checks, rips out four from the back. Afterwards, my mother spends hours in that trailer, tapping the ledger with her pencil, trying to balance an unbalanceable account. Then, at night, my father comes home hopelessly late for dinner, his breath burning of alcohol and sex, jovial, unbundling his treasures, an antique cannon for him, ballerina dolls for us, a dress for my mother.

My father says we were rich. My mother says it was a time of poverty and deprivation.

Another memory, this mostly mine. The women are gathered together, practicing some variation of talk therapy, while my father shows all the boys and men a film. I, as usual, choose activities not by gender but by their pleasure and power quotient. I remember the darkened cabin, the crowded living room, everyone sprawled on the floor, the click, hiss of the film as it slides through the projector. My father is showing *Culloden*. He must have been there some of the time, because I remember him explaining the film to me. The massacre of the Scots by the British in 1746. Farmers and little boys armed with pitchforks and axes up against a well-trained army. They march in the old style, coming together to the rhythm of fife and drum. The Scots are massacred. I watch as a little boy is shot, he falls, he hangs on to his father's coat, but the father keeps marching, dragging his son behind him.

The phone rings, and my father comes back and says the main house is on fire.

Then we are all down the hill, ringing the burning building. Someone grips my hand, holds my little sister in her arms. Not my mother. The low-slung clouds are full of snow, but the air is warm. Ash falls on a slant. A house fire has a deep voice, a roar that causes panic, makes it hard to reason. Is everyone accounted for? Where is the dog? I hear that my father is looking for Giovanni in the burning house. Finally, my father stumbles out. Later, Giovanni is found asleep in a loft in the bunker.

The pigs are penned close to the back of the main house. They are going berserk, squealing and throwing themselves against the chicken wire as if trying to tumble themselves into the blaze. I hope the fence will hold. Then Doug is in the office, hurling copying machines and typewriters out the window. I remember seeing his dark hair backlit by the flames. People are yelling, Get out.

I remember the grey, grainy photograph in the local paper. The picture is mainly of billowing smoke, a mushroom cloud that hides the noise and the light and the fear.

On one of our car rides my mother says she thinks my father started the fire for the insurance. It's too much of a coincidence — every person safely away from the main house. I try to imagine him planning it. I can picture him walking quickly through the building in his dark blue jeans, his work shirt, his Mexican silver and turquoise belt, gripping a red gas can in his silver-ringed fingers. Trailing gas onto the green rug of the meeting room, my mother's desk cluttered with bills, the rumpled bed next to the tropical fish tank, over flannel shirts and jeans and work boots, a room smelling thickly of personal belongings before it begins to smell of gas. Is he tempted to save anything? Or is his soul thrumming with rightness? My father illustrates natural law. Destruction does not feel like disorder, but like an ordering, an illustration of the way of all matter.

Did he burn it for the money? I remember him talking to Brad about financial problems at the school. They are sitting at our long, scarred table in the log cabin. My father gets up, lights a candle and places it in the middle of the table. He opens his battered wallet, takes out a fifty-dollar bill. He turns the bill over in his hands, then dips the edge in the candle flame. He holds on to a corner, watches it blacken down to ash. I remember Brad's nervous laugh.

My mother says the main house was underinsured, and with the cost of replacing the office and kitchen equipment, they ended up losing money.

I'm a kid, we're walking along a street of a small town in Vermont, my temporarily nuclear family. My parents are arguing about finances. You can always get money if you need it, my father says. He reaches into his pocket and pulls out a handful of coins. He flings them away. The silver and copper spangle in the sun, then chime onto the street. I want to run to the gutter and gather the money up, but my father holds my hand tight and won't let me go.

My father desires violently, but briefly. This much has poured through his fingers: five hundred acres of Adirondack wilderness, scores of antique weapons, a half-track, a yacht, a hotel and captain's house in Nova Scotia; homes in Boulder, New York City, Washington, Florida, Westchester, Denver, Maine; a Saab, an MG, scores of friends and lovers, five wives, five daughters, a son. I don't think he misses any of it much. He gives easily—his sword, the sweater he is wearing, the photograph framed on his wall. I have never heard him wish for anything back. My father says you can distill Buddhism down to one basic tenet, a quote from the Buddha himself, Do not cling.

My father and I have not clung to each other, but we call sometimes. I have seen him maybe ten times in the last twenty years.

A few years before his death, Rinpoche tells my father it is time for him to leave the fold, to make his own way in the world. My father says Rinpoche thought he should begin his own religion, the Crazy Heart Lineage. Just after I graduate from college, in 1986, I visit my father in Boston, where he has taken up his mother's profession, serving. My father is living with his fifth wife and sixth child, a baby boy, in the servant's quarters in an aristocratic apartment on Beacon Hill. He is impersonating a British butler to the hilt. He wears expensive, tweedy suits and has purchased a bowler hat.

After a year or two in Boston, my father moves his family to Manhattan to buttle for Bill Cosby. They live in a two-room apartment, he carries a beeper and smokes expensive cigars. His apartment has a Buddhist shrine with a gilded box that contains a pair of Rinpoche's shoes. On the wall is a framed photograph of my stepmother, the summer she was a Las Vegas showgirl, feathers coming out of her head. Another photograph of her as a ballet dancer in gauzy tutu. His family seems isolated in New York, holed up in the small apartment with videos and sake. They think the culture is close to its breaking point and are making plans to buy a farm in Nova Scotia and raise goats.

My husband and I visit, sleep on the futon couch and my father brings me tea in the morning. During the course of my three or four visits, I fall in love with my father's three-year-old son, who has huge blue eyes, likes glamorous costumes, dancing and chasing pigeons when he gets the chance. He follows us to the elevator, begging us not to leave. I have fantasies of adopting him.

Soon after, my husband and I have our own son, and we visit my father in Washington, D.C. He is separated from his last wife and butlering for a couple in the Watergate building. My father, elegant and gentle, hands us wine glasses, cooks good Indian food. The apartment is done up in grey-green velvet and has a panoramic view of the Potomac. In the sitting room, one side of the wall is covered in photographs of my father's bosses with various presidents, the other wall is devoted to pug art. There are two old wheezing pug dogs. When they grow excited, they faint. My father seems to like them. He sits with one on his lap, stroking it, getting up for more alcohol or more expensive chocolate.

His bosses are on vacation. He tells me he has converted them to Buddhism. When they were in a car accident the year before, the officer at the scene wondered why my father, the butler, was sitting in the backseat while the employer drove. My father replied, I was fatigued.

My father lifts up my son, gives him a beautiful gift, carries him over to the window to look. Afterwards, he sends my son an eight-by-ten photograph of himself in his orange robes. He writes over it, *This is part of your heritage, too. Love, your grandfather.*

Over these visits, and during our phone conversations, I keep it light. Sometimes my father tries to say something serious, says, I know I was a bad father. But I answer ironically, slip away.

He calls regularly these last years: How are you, Honey, always sounding tired and kind. But I'm wary of getting too close. My proximity to his fearsome reputation protected me in the valley, and I kept enough distance between us so that I felt safe from him. I've been fencing with him like this my whole life.

Recently, he retired from buttling to devote all his energies to the Crazy Heart Lineage. My father has a business card that reads Celtic Buddhist Shaman. He gives religious talks at colleges and conferences in his orange robes and turquoise necklaces. He's working on raising funds to build his first dharma center.

When he recalls his life, Buddha figures at all the crucial junctures. He remembers that as a child his family ate at a Chinese restaurant on the day after Christmas. There, he fell in love with the smiling golden Buddha at the entrance. A few weeks after the Christmas of his eighth year, the girl next door died of diphtheria, and then my father came down with it. In bed, he had a fever dream in which the golden Buddha revealed itself to him. Rays shot from the Buddha's heart and entered my father. His fever broke.

He says that he didn't like killing animals at the valley, that the slaughtering depressed him. When I tell him he seemed to enjoy it, he says it was just an act.

And of course, he remembers the Buddha my mother chucked at him on his final departure.

*

It's summer 2000, Bill Clinton is still president, a child of the sixties himself, sexy, warmhearted, with a few moral complications. There are no walls in the White House, so we all know what he does with his cigars. Me, I live in California, in the near future. We have rolling brownouts, houses cost a million dollars and people sublet their closets. It never snows.

I live in a condo. I have a boy, a girl, a husband, a career, some friends. The structure of my life is not shocking in the least. I teach at a liberal university, and many of my students are children of hippies. They tend to be careful, lightly ironic, slightly morally anguished people.

We fly back east for a visit. Here, so near the end of the story, is a perfect place for a reunion, a grand reconciliation. But that's not possible. Instead we make two visits, one to my mother, one to my father.

While my husband goes on a week's bike ride, the kids and I travel to visit my mother and Paul in the Adirondacks. (My mother and Paul have been together for twenty-five years.) When my sister graduated from high school, my mother and Paul left Vermont and moved back to the valley. They are alone here, in the log cabin, with their books, their computers, their fax and their two phone lines. Paul commutes to work, and my mother is a human service consultant, traveling by plane and car, talking for hours on the phone.

But often the phone lines go dead. Sometimes in spring the road floods and they are marooned for weeks. Once they canoed down the road to get the mail. My father wonders how they can spend their lives like hermits. Don't they get bored? he asks me.

Maybe they're still recovering from sensory overload. They

never seem bored to me. They are full of enthusiasms. During my childhood, my mother was too busy with people to notice nature, but now she sits in the woods by the hour, just watching birds and squirrels about their daily business. A few years ago, Paul shot a bear, and my mother prided herself on using every bit. She gave me a little baby food jar of bear grease to shine my shoes. She reads Annie Dillard, brings home a fox skull, boils it and sets it on the mantle. The wild world makes her cry with happiness.

Paul likes computers and tractors, and he's a Judaic scholar. Like my father, my mother and Paul have slowly become religious fanatics. My mother and Paul are reconstructionist Jews — taking an old religion and making it new. Religion is a shared vision, a communal experience of renewal and transcendence. They're still up to their old tricks.

They spent last year in Israel. In the photographs she sends back, my mother looks electric. She writes that it is Succoth, the autumn harvest holiday. The Bible demands that you be happy for seven straight days. Not difficult for her. They have made the traditional little lean-to on their roof in Jerusalem. They have hung pomegranates, pineapples, tiny white lights, palm fronds. They sleep in it at night. One early morning, my mother wakes to a hummingbird flitting round the fruit. My mother says a prayer of thanksgiving. Then the bird shits on her pillow. My mother just laughs and says another prayer of thanksgiving.

My sister says my mother is so happy it makes her queasy. Shit just doesn't get to her, my sister says.

At least now she acknowledges the shit, I say.

*

My children asleep in the car, I drive the two-mile dirt road to the valley. I pass the twin waterfalls where the bus went off the road all those years ago. I have an unwelcome fantasy of careening off the road. Our car begins to sink. I roll down the windows, unbuckle my seatbelt, reach back for the children. If only I act decisively, I can save us. Muddy green water is gushing in through the open windows. I hold my children by the arms, no maybe a better grip would be the clothes, or even the hair. I tell them to take a deep breath. We swim through the window, and I push them above me towards the air.

I decide this fantasy comes from anxiety over the fact that I haven't seen Mom, Paul or my sister since they read my memoir. On the phone, my mother said she loved it, but now, I'm worried that it will bring about some unforeseen, irreparable damage. I remember the fire-haired painter who caused the bus to crash.

My sister has driven across the bridge from Vermont where she has her own ceramic business, and pulls into the log cabin driveway at the same time we do. She climbs down from her jacked-up black Ford pickup. She is tan, skinny, has short bleached hair and a nose ring. She wears a minidress, a suede jacket and platform shoes. Her kiss on my cheek is light and dry.

My mother suggests we all go to the lake. My sister nixes this. My sister has learned to speak up, with a vengeance. She cut Dad off years ago, said she couldn't take his manipulative ways. Nobody calls her Beky, she's Bekah now. She doesn't want anything to do with the baby sister routine. Don't mess with her.

Now, she announces that she and I are going into town to buy her a spare tire. Whatever you say. We leave my mother to baby-sit my kids and head out. She throws the platform shoes on the floor of the truck to drive barefoot. I watch her elegant silver-ringed fingers on the steering wheel, her elegant silver-ringed toes on the gas pedal.

You're lucky you didn't make me into a whining little victim in that memoir, she says.

She tells me that Maddy, the ex–valley student, found her name in the phonebook and has been calling her as much as six times a day. She leaves messages for Bekah to tell my mother that she is deeply regretful of the incident when she stole a gun and threatened to kill Les and his family. Maddy says she hadn't meant to scare anyone, she just wanted to hunt deer and live off the land. When my sister played the last message, it said, Beky, tell your mother that I was very disturbed when your father burnt down the main house, bought a yacht with the money and ran away with a fifteen-year-old student. Tell your mother that if she can forgive him, she can forgive me.

How does she know about that? I ask.

Why does she think Mom's forgiven him? Bekah says.

Bekah tells me about a dream she had recently. I was walking across this icy bridge in the winter with a bunch of people, she says. I had rubber boots on. People started to fall in the water. The snow was really slippery. I was scared that I was going to fall, so I threw myself onto my back to steady myself, but I slipped into the water. My boots began to fill. As I went down, I saw these other people. Some were drowning and dead. Some were trying to swim. I thought, I could drown.

And then I felt this swelling thought: No. I swam really fast to the top. I pulled my rubber boots off and burst out of the water. I screamed to the other people, Take your boots and clothes off, they're going to drag you down, and I said, Swim.

Bekah gives me a smile at once self-mocking and triumphant. Put that in your memoir, she says.

After my sister leaves, my mother, my kids and I go for a walk across the valley. The remaining two A-frames are rented to artists and writers for the summer. The valley looks less like a valley these days, it's filling with fast-growing trees, willows and poplars. The beaver have flooded one field, our neighbors have planted spruce all over another. Paul is doing his best to keep the trees back. He's mowing on his newest toy, a red Farm-all tractor. We can hear the rumble. My mother is her usual chatty, ebullient self, praising the beauty of my children, the beauty of the green valley as we swat mosquitoes.

We take the two-track that leads into the woods where the Celts once made their fort. The kids run ahead and behind, discovering sticks and newts. I haven't seen my mother in the year she was away in Israel, and I can only take her in glances. Her image is doubled. On one long slender neck waves the mother of my childhood, the one I adored with a physical passion. This is the one I expect to act as my moral compass, to wrap me in her smooth arms and press me to her perfect breasts, to croon, Don't worry, we're on the right track, the one who lives only for my pleasure and comfort. And of course this new one, grey-streaked short hair, elegant bifocals, bird thin, this one who seems to have distilled down to passion and bones.

My mother and I have talked about building a playhouse for the kids on the property. Now, here it is, a surprise, under a little spruce tree. The kids rush inside. I duck my head and follow. In my imagination, the playhouse had linoleum on the floor, gingham curtains, the spotless, ordered little house I yearned for as a child. But the house my mother designed is made from wood left over from the old valley construction projects. It has wood and cinder-block beds covered in Indian print bedspreads, raw board shelves. Stupid of me to think my mother would have made a miniature suburban Eden. That's just what she's never been interested in.

My kids seem delighted with their rustic cabin in the woods. They begin to play pioneer.

My mother and I sit down in the grassy clearing, a few feet away. Ants cruise up our ankles.

Isn't this the old dump? I say.

Yep. Guess what's under here?

What?

Bo's trailer. Paul and Laurie's VW Bug.

I study the slightly humpy terrain. There is no indication of the massive relics that lie below.

We talk a little about my sister. My sister in some ways is more like my parents, forging ahead in the avant-garde with her transgender and transsexual politics. She's managed to find a lifestyle that my mother and Paul, although supportive, don't really understand. At her transgendered wedding a few years ago, she wore white, her transgendered partner wore a suit, and though born a woman, thinks of himself as a man.

Do you think it's good that Bekah doesn't ever talk to your father? My mother asks.

I don't answer her. I don't know. Sometimes I think that I have come much farther than my sister with my relationship with my father, sometimes I think I haven't even begun. You know what's interesting, I say out loud. Dad's mother left him out of her will? his father abandoned him and now his daughter won't speak to him. It's like everyone is trying to erase him. I don't quite have the nerve to say, And you pretend he never existed. I'm looking for some sympathy, but I'm looking in the wrong place.

The way he pretended his mother was dead. She shakes her head.

Buddhism has really changed him, I say. He's always kind on the phone.

Really? She sounds skeptical.

He says nice things about you.

He does?

He says when he met you, you were the most beautiful smart woman he'd ever met. He says the only thing wrong with your marriage was that he wanted to sleep with other women and you didn't like that. He says he can understand that.

Maybe he's finally grown a conscience. My mother isn't buying any of this.

He didn't do anything that bad, I say, defensive.

Are you kidding? She leans towards me. He did terrible things. He hit students. He slept with the students, talk about an abuse of power. He was having sex with an eighteen-year-old girl and invited her into our home for the weekend. I cooked for them. Once he rowed Kitty and Ann out to an island and they ran around with their clothes off.

Did they have sex?

I don't know, probably, probably he tried to.

How do you know about this?

He must have told me.

I don't say anything, just watch my kids. My head feels hot and empty.

Was that hard for you to hear? she says.

I don't know. I want to know everything, part of me does, but some things don't seem appropriate to tell a daughter.

You've heard all those stories before.

No, I haven't.

We had a good time on trips, she tries lamely. We took great trips.

Mom, you just demonize him so you don't have to take responsibility for any of it.

You're right.

It's hard when you always make him into some kind of devil, because I know I'm a lot like him. It used to make me feel like I was Rosemary's baby or something.

That was a mistake. I regret that. Paul called me a moralistic son of a bitch the other day.

I smile.

It's true. I'm not that easy to live with. I'm a moralistic son of a bitch.

I can tell she likes saying that.

She says, I'm not worried about the memoir. I've let it go. But there's just one thing that really bothers me.

My heart clenches. What?

You wrote that when your father left, I wiped my nose on the bedspread. I would never do that. I always use tissues. The bedspread. That's disgusting.

A week later, we meet up with my husband and visit my father in New England, where he has reinvented himself all over again. He and his youngest son, who is now twelve and spending the summer with him, are living in a farmhouse in a small town. My father answers the door wearing a white dress shirt, sleeves rolled up. He has on black pants, little glasses, his long grey hair in a silver barrette. He is bent slightly at the waist, that stance that I associate with the game of impersonating a butler or a soldier, slightly mocking, halfway between a bow and a salute. He's acquired a dental bridge, and his new teeth are pretty, white and straight (what big teeth you have, Granny).

His things are still in boxes after his move from Washington, D.C. The farmhouse looks the way a New England farmhouse ought to look, with wide floorboards, brick fireplace, colonial-like furniture. He is still playing pilgrim.

They have a little yapping dog, a corgi, that leaps at my children. My two-year-old blond daughter spends the afternoon in my lap. My father, who has never met her before, says, She's gorgeous, watch out, she'll drive the boys mad. He pays only glancing attention to my five-year-old son.

He makes us lamb and mint sauce for dinner. He tells us his summer plans: an African safari, then Irish Buddhists are sponsoring a two-month residency for him outside of Dublin. Maybe my half sisters Sophie and Tillie will meet him over there. Tillie is beautiful, he says, but Sophie looks like us. He shakes his head.

My younger brother looks more like Robert Redford playing Gatsby than like us, in his preppie clothes and blond twenties-style haircut. He orders my father around, tells him what to wear, how to fix his tea, Sleepy Time steeped for five minutes, one spoonful of honey.

My father asks me to braid his hair for him. It's nice hair, thick and silver. But immediately after I am done, my brother tells him it looks too weird. Wear it in the barrette, the length is less noticeable. My father complies.

My father smiles ruefully. This is my karma. I neglected all my other children so I've ended up serving the little prince in my old age.

My little brother does remind me of a somnambulant prince. I'm not sure what to say to him. We talk about home decorating, he shows me a photograph in his favorite magazine, *Architectural Digest*, a monumental room with pillars and drapes. He is a boy of beautiful armor. I don't try to get beyond it except to say, If you ever need anything—just as my father used to say to me.

As my father brings my little brother his tea the way he likes it, I say, My father wasn't a butler.

What was your father? my father asks. It's after dinner. My children are asleep upstairs, my half brother has just taken his tea and magazine up to his room. My father, my husband and I sit in wooden chairs around the kitchen table.

My father was a wild man, I answer.

Insane, he agrees. My father begins to talk a little about the death of Rinpoche, his beloved teacher. My father says people were always upset that Rinpoche slept with his students, upset about all the wild things he did. My father says once Rinpoche confessed that he had pushed things too far.

So Rinpoche apologized? I asked.

No, he didn't apologize. He said he pushed things too far, but if he hadn't I wouldn't be where I am today.

I get it, I say. We start talking about the valley school.

I suppose we helped some of the students, he says. Do you think any of them had any fun? I was too interested in myself then, to notice.

My husband and father talk. My father likes the fact that my husband cooks well, keeps an orderly home. If you leave Micah, he says to my husband, come live with me.

At one point my husband mentions that I don't like anyone telling me what to do.

Why not? my father asks me.

I shrug. Do you like being told what to do? I ask.

I've been a servant for twenty years, my dear, my father says sharply.

How did you do it?

He gets up and rummages through a box, pulls out a long silver sword. I call this my ego cutter.

We talk a little more, he says, Thank you for sending me your memoir. It's great.

He's already told me this on the phone, and I just repeat, Thanks, Dad.

Except, I didn't burn down the main house.

Tell me what happened then, I say.

We were up at the log cabin, he begins. Doug called and said smoke was coming out of somewhere in the main house.

I got down there. We each took a fire extinguisher and went upstairs. There was smoke, but we couldn't find the fire. Then I saw smoke leaking out of a trap door in the ceiling of the upstairs bathroom. I still think that if I hadn't opened that trap door ... But I did.

Flames and smoke burst out. Let's get the hose hooked up, I yelled. We ran downstairs, got everyone together. We formed a fire brigade. But it was ridiculous. At some point I gave up, said, Let the place burn.

But then we realized a student was missing. I went inside to search the house. I went upstairs, I was moving from bed to bed, the smoke was very thick. I realized I had to get out of there, but I couldn't find the door, I couldn't breathe. I almost lost it.

The state police ended up saying that it was a grease fire, from a plywood vent over the stove.

Do you think Doug started the fire? I ask.

No, I don't think Doug burnt it down.

What else, Dad?

There was a lot of smoke.

That night, my father gives us his room and camps out on the couch downstairs. My husband goes out to the car to retrieve our suitcase. My children are asleep in the bed as I walk quietly into the dark bedroom upstairs. I glance down at the old-fashioned metal floor grate. I crouch. There, directly below me, uncostumed, unmasked, is my father. He is asleep with the light on, his long silver hair spread around him on the couch, his arms crossed over his pale chest. From this vantage point, I am free to study him. Has he really become an ego-less, gentle Buddhist? Has meditation channeled all that rage? My husband, a man of science, says that we are constantly replacing the atoms in our bodies, so that every nine months we reinvent ourselves. Even writing a memoir cannot bring us back. We are already someone else.

So, this is the way it's turned out, I think. When I first began writing, I planned to record a communal memoir. I spent hours and hours taping conversations with the main characters. I spent hours meticulously transcribing them. But slowly, draft on draft, I took over. I, Boadicea warrior queen, have usurped all the stories and made them my own.

But I could have gone even farther, changed everything. Would you believe that one muggy afternoon I chanced upon Doug and Ann abusing Bo in the hayloft? There was a pitchfork leaning against the wall. I raised it above my head, stabbed them both again and again. Then, Bo and I jumped out of the loft, landed in a pile of dusty hay and ran.

Remember that lamp fire I started with my handmade book? That was actually the fire that burnt the main house down. It was me all the time.

I don't believe it, either, not quite. You see, there are rules to this. Aren't there?

I hear a soft knock on the front door downstairs, another. My husband calls out, Hello? Can someone open the door? My father doesn't stir. Did he lock my husband out on purpose, a joke? Is he feigning sleep? I hear my husband knocking now on the living room window.

Suddenly my father's lids slide back. He seems to be staring right at me. I'm not sure, and I don't move. Outside, my husband calls my father's name and then my own.

Maybe it's time for the warrior queen to make her move.

acknowledgments

Gratitude is due:

To the Blue Mountain Center, for time

To the Saltonstall Foundation for the Arts, for financial support

To Sunderland Cottages on Paradox Lake, for rest and relaxation (I'm so glad I rediscovered you on the web)

To Farm and Wilderness, for sanctuary

To Esther and Samson, for playing themselves to perfection

To Bob, for geology, geography and great cooking

To Jeff Furman and "Bo," for stories

To Peter Gizzi, Karen Yamashita, Deborah Tannen, Alison Lurie, Michael Koch, Juan Poblete, Paul Cody, Liz Holmes, Brian Hall, Polly Wagner, Wm Levine, Liz Willis, Bob Lautenslager, Malia Mulder Wollan, Jennifer Gonzalez, Susan McClosky, my parents and sister, Counterpoint and The Joy Harris Agency, for support in the making of the manuscript

To Joy Harris and Dawn Seferian, for excellence

To Juan, for opening the window

Printed in the United States
by Baker & Taylor Publisher Services